If your enemy is secure at all points, be prepared for him. If he is in superior strength, evade him. If your opponent is temperamental, seek to irritate him. Pretend to be weak, that he may grow arrogant. If he is taking his ease, give him no rest. If his forces are united, separate them. Attack him where he is unprepared, appear where you are not expected.

Sun Tzu, 6th century BC Chinese General

KEEP YOUR FRIENDS CLOSE

TONY MILLINGTON

Published in 2022 by Dark Edge Press.

Y Bwthyn
Caerleon road,
Newport,
Wales.

www.darkedgepress.co.uk

Text copyright © 2022 Tony Millington

Cover Design: Jamie Curtis

Cover Photography: Canva

The moral right of Tony Millington to be identified as the author of this work has been asserted in accordance with the Copyright, Designs and Patents Act 1988.

All rights reserved, including the right to reproduce this book, or portions thereof in any form. No part of this text may be reproduced, transmitted, downloaded, decompiled, reverse engineered, stored, or introduced into any information storage and retrieval system by any means, whether electronic or mechanical without the express written permission of the author.

This is a work of fiction. Names, characters, places, incidents and dialogues are products of the author's imagination or are used fictitiously. Any resemblance to actual people, living or dead, events or locales is entirely coincidental.

A CIP catalogue record for this book is available from the British Library.

ISBN (eBook): B09H4PCY8Z
ISBN: (Paperback): 979-8-4214-0344-9

CONTENTS

PROLOGUE

CHAPTER ONE

CHAPTER TWO

CHAPTER THREE

CHAPTER FOUR

CHAPTER FIVE

CHAPTER SIX

CHAPTER SEVEN

CHAPTER EIGHT

CHAPTER NINE

CHAPTER TEN

CHAPTER ELEVEN

CHAPTER TWELVE

CHAPTER THIRTEEN

CHAPTER FOURTEEN

CHAPTER FIFTEEN

CHAPTER SIXTEEN

CHAPTER SEVENTEEN

CHAPTER EIGHTEEN

CHAPTER NINETEEN

CHAPTER TWENTY

CHAPTER TWENTY-ONE

CHAPTER TWENTY-TWO

CHAPTER TWENTY-THREE

CHAPTER TWENTY-FOUR

CHAPTER TWENTY-FOUR

CHAPTER TWENTY-FIVE

CHAPTER TWENTY-SIX

CHAPTER TWENTY-SEVEN

CHAPTER TWENTY-NINE

CHAPTER THIRTY

CHAPTER THIRTY-ONE

CHAPTER THIRTY-TWO

CHAPTER THIRTY-THREE

CHAPTER THIRTY-FOUR

CHAPTER THIRTY-FIVE

CHAPTER THIRTY-SIX

CHAPTER THIRTY-SEVEN

CHAPTER THIRTY-EIGHT

CHAPTER THIRTY-NINE

CHAPTER FORTY

CHAPTER FORTY-ONE

CHAPTER FORTY-TWO

CHAPTER FORTY-THREE

CHAPTER FORTY-FOUR

CHAPTER FORTY-FIVE

CHAPTER FORTY-SIX

CHAPTER FORTY-SEVEN

CHAPTER FORTY-EIGHT

CHAPTER FORTY-NINE

CHAPTER FIFTY

CHAPTER FIFTY-ONE

CHAPTER FIFTY-TWO

CHAPTER FIFTY-THREE

CHAPTER FIFTY-FOUR

CHAPTER FIFTY-FIVE

CHAPTER FIFTY-SIX

EPILOGUE

PROLOGUE

Monteith was glad his day had finished. Matthews had been pressing him again to get information on the Russell's, but he was getting nowhere with just being a patron of the casino. They kept their business and private lives separate. Trying to make a jerk like Matthews understand that was impossible.

Mac had confirmed the identity of the river body as Duncan Healey, adding another murder to Susan's charges of accessory to the fact.

Crompton was facing trial for the murder of Littlewood. He was being kept under close supervision in prison.

DCI Tanya Wright had come in and had hit the ground running. She was fair but tough when needed to be.

There was talk that as they didn't officially have one a Detective Inspector was needing promoting.

Watson had gone into town to meet his wife and children for a meal. Monteith, at least could relax for a couple of days before re-entering the madhouse that was the Criminal Detective Agency.

Walking towards his BMW Series 1, Monteith flicked through the text messages that had been left on his iPhone as he approached his car.

Two men dressed in dark clothing stepped out in front of him.

One of them smashed a right-handed punch into Monteith's face. The force of which sent him bouncing off the front wing of the car next to him. One of the men forced a hessian bag over his head and bound his hands behind his back with Ty-Raps before he had time to yell for help.

'What the hell? Who are you?' Monteith mumbled, feeling the full force of a kick to his stomach, which knocked the wind out of his lungs.

He heard a van pull up next to him and doors opening. Then he was hoisted off the ground and thrown into the back of the van. The doors slammed shut, the engine revved, then whoever was driving the van moved off.

'Got you,' Allan Russell said.

He sat in his car and watched the event unfolding from afar. He waited till the van had cleared the car park before he followed it at a safe distance.

Jimmy Russell was sampling one of the finest scotches in his collection, a Highland Park, distilled in 1974, and bottled in 2006. Only one hundred and forty-one bottles had ever been made.

A notification on his mobile phone disrupted him. It was a text message. He read it with a smile.

Your package has been collected.

CHAPTER ONE

MONDAY EVENING 6.15 p.m.

Detective Sergeant Terry Watson had just finished his shift and had joined his family in celebrating their son, Jason's, 12th birthday with a meal out. They were at the new dessert restaurant, which had only recently opened up in the city centre. Terry would have preferred something like a Steakhouse, Domino's or Frankie & Benny's, but this was what Jason wanted.

It was the first time in months that they had been able to do something like this as a family due to the high caseload at the Criminal Detective Agency of the West Ravenswood Police Force. They'd just finalised the paperwork on a case involving a serial killer. The offender having been killed himself by the former Detective Chief Inspector Kenneth Crompton during a standoff at the top of a multi-storey car park. The DCI was charged with murder and was being held without bail pending his trial.

The restaurant was packed and humming with noise from the early evening trade. The Watsons: Terry, his wife Sally, and their three children, Simon, Rachael and of course Jason were given a table at the front of the restaurant.

'Just grin and bear it,' Sally said in his ear, as the kids were busy picking what they were going to have.

'Hope you have something better to eat back home after this?' Terry replied.

'I'm sure I can whip something up for you, dear.' Sally had a glint in her eye. 'Right who is having what?' Sally said, looking at the three excited faces of their children.

'Can I have a hot fudge sundae?' Jason piped up eagerly.

'A knickerbocker glory, please Mum,' Simon added with glee.

Rachael was still trying to decide. A study of concentration on her face. Sally leaned over. 'What do you fancy?'

'I'm not sure . . . erm, banana split?' she said, looking at her mum wearing a big grin and rosy cheeks.

'Banana split it is then.'

Sally's phone started to ring as the waiter came over to take their orders. She answered it while Terry spoke to the waiter.

'Hello?' Sally struggled to hear the person on the other end with all the noise in the restaurant.

'Hi, Sally it's Katie. Sorry to ring you but is Terry with you?' Katie was the wife of Terry's partner, DS Keith Monteith.

'Yes, Can you speak up I can hardly hear you.' Sally tried to block out what noise she could.

'Keith's not home yet. I was wondering if Terry knew where he was.' Katie was sounding worried.

'I will pass you across,' Sally shouted before giving the phone to Terry who was wondering who it was. She mouthed Katie's name.

Terry took the phone and went outside. To get out of way of the people wandering around, he nipped down a side alley.

'Hi Katie, I can hear you now. Jason says thanks for his present by the way. No Keith was still at the office when I left . . . he was finishing off some paperwork and talking to the boss.' Terry's own phone started to ring. He looked at it seeing it was his new boss, DCI Tanya Wright.

'Listen, Katie, I am sure he will be home soon, you know what he is like for forgetting the time. Listen I have our boss on my phone, I will ask her if he has left yet and get back to you.'

Terry changed phones.

'Hi, boss.'

'Sorry to pull you away from Jason's party, but can you get back here now. We have a big problem.' With that, she was gone.

Terry was left standing, bewildered. No inklings as to why he had to go back, just get back here now. He returned to the restaurant and sat down, handing Sally's phone back to her. He whispered to her that he had to go back. Her face was like thunder but she had got used to things like this. It was part of the job. He said what he could to Simon, Rachael and especially to Jason to placate the situation he had been put in. But even though they had got used to daddy disappearing, it was always hard to do.

Ten minutes later and out of breath, Watson was in the CDA office after running most of the way back.

The CDA team composed of Watson, Sergeant Karl Lorimer, and DCI Tanya Wright were looking at CCTV footage of the car park at the back of their headquarters. They had been joined by the Custody Sergeant and by Detective Superintendent Matthews. The footage showed Monteith exiting the custody door, head down, looking at his phone. Then he was confronted by two men who attacked him and bundled him into the back of a dark coloured van and took off.

'Why did no-one go to help him!?' DCI Wright shouted at the Custody Sergeant.

'We were busy. All the cells are full down there and it was kicking off. The first thing anyone knew was when I glanced at the CCTV camera and saw Keith being chucked into the van. By the time we got out there the van was gone,' The Custody Sergeant replied.

'Right, we have all squad cars on the lookout for the van with an approach with caution order. We don't want to put Monteith in any bigger harm than he looks like he is already in,' Wright informed the team. 'A call has gone out for the helicopter to give us eyes in the sky.'

'Who's he pissed off lately?' Matthews was as tactful as ever with his remarks.

'No-one!' Watson turned on him. 'After you ordered him to get close to Jimmy Russell or lose his job he has tried to get his life back together.' Watson was full of anger. 'He has kept his head down and got on with his work.'

'Watson!' DCI Wright said in a stern voice. 'My office now!'

'Just remember who you're talking to DS Watson,' Matthews reminded him who was in charge. Watson went to say something else but caught Wright shaking her head as if to say don't try it, causing Watson to storm off.

'I suggest you keep your troops in check DCI Wright.' Matthews pointed a finger at her before turning and marching out of the door back to his ivory office on the top floor. He very rarely made an appearance at the coal face of policing, but when he did his attitude towards everyone put their backs up.

He was the head and he made sure people knew about it.

Watson was looking out of the window at the city centre when Wright entered. He turned to face her as she closed the door.

'Don't say anything,' Wright jumped in. 'Why in God's name did you fly off the handle like that?'

'Matthews is a moron. He does not have a clue what we do down here and what we go through. Having a go at Keith like that was out of order.'

'I know and I feel the same way but shouting in his face like that does not help. I was warned when I took this job what he was like, and he does have his head up his arse, stuck up there in his office. But there are ways and means to keep him off our backs.'

Watson started to smile at the way Wright described Matthews. They both looked at each other sniggering before laughter filled the room. Wright had been a breath of fresh air since she was brought in as the new DCI. Everyone could have a joke with her but when there was work to be done she made sure they were doing it. And when their work was called into question she backed them to the full.

Calming down, Wright continued. 'Now I know Terry that Keith is your partner and a good friend, but let's start to think rationally. Keith does have a not so clean past, so is there anything which has gone on recently which may have led to him being bundled into a van like we saw. What about the Russells?'

Watson sat down. 'Abduction is not normally their style. Keith paid his dues to them before you took over. Intimidation and power building have been their style, but they have kept a low profile lately. Not putting their heads above the parapet. Keith heard the last time he was up there they were expanding their casino business. Adding possibly a so-called private gentleman's club.'

'Do they need planning permission for that?'

'Who knows? And will they care if they do? They will get around it somehow. Just mention the Russell name and watch everyone either run a mile or lick their shoes.'

Lorimer knocked on the door before entering. 'Sorry to interrupt, nothing from the squad cars but the helicopter crew has just reported seeing a large vehicle on fire out by the landfill site. With it getting dark they cannot be certain if it's the one we are after. Fire engines just arrived. They will continue searching unless told to stand down.'

'Hang on Karl. Terry, you and Karl go and check that out and report back. We need to be certain it's our van or rule it out.' DCI Wright followed them back into the main office. 'Take a print-out of the CCTV picture of the van we are after.'

Putting on his jacket Watson added, 'What about Keith's wife? When are we going to tell her that her husband's gone missing? She rang me just before you did asking if I knew where he was.'

'Check the van first, and then we can tell her of the situation. Can your wife go round there just to check on her and so there is someone with her if we have news?'

'I'll give her a call.'

CHAPTER TWO

MONDAY 8 p.m.

Watson and Lorimer arrived at the piece of wasteland by the landfill site in their blues and twos. Both had been listening to the airwaves for updates, keeping their chat to a minimum. Not wanting to think of what they could find when they got there. Watson rang and updated Sally asking her to go sit with Katie.

The van was smouldering and thick smoke hung overhead like another layer to the cloud formation in the night sky, mixed with the stench of the fermenting waste. Both covered their mouths with hankies and showed their ID cards to the PC on duty, who directed them over to the head of the station's fire watch.

'What brings you lot out to a van fire?' The fire chief looked surprised.

'One of our colleagues has gone missing, taken in a van similar to what's left of this one,' Watson said sombrely.

'And you think they're in there? Jesus!' the chief was taken aback. 'If they were there's no hope for them. It was well ablaze when we arrived. We are dampening down but we can check soon. Just give us some time.'

Not long after they arrived Watson and Lorimer were able to approach the burnt out remains. It had gone from being a hardworking and dependable transportation vehicle to a white husk. Nothing of significance looked to have remained, colour, number plates, any identification.

'Fire was definitely started with an accelerant. Probably petrol,' the Station Watch Chief confirmed. 'But that's not what you are here for.'

Watson and Lorimer were shown around the van, keeping at a safe distance in case of flare-ups, to where the sliding side door was. It was open.

'Whoever did this doused the insides of the van with the petrol before setting it alight. There looks to be no body inside the van. Even with a fire of this intensity, you would still see remnants.'

Lorimer returned to the car to report their findings back to DCI Wright, while Watson took one of the fireman's torches to see what was left inside – which was not much. The fire had done its job. He could still feel the heat coming off the van and the air around it.

'Let us know if you come across anything of interest.' Watson handed back the torch.

'There is this, which we picked up from outside of the van.' The Fire Chief handed half a number plate to Watson. 'Don't know if it came from the van or from another vehicle. The front number plate had gone up in flames.'

'That's not enough to do a PNC check.' The plate only had AC15 on it. 'A lot of cars and vans would have the same on their plates. Bag it and give it to forensics when they arrive, thanks.'

-X-

Lorimer dropped Watson off at Monteith's house around 9 p.m. after informing the DCI. Sally was already there. The children from both families were upstairs playing. Katie had been looking out of the living room window and had opened the front door as soon as Watson had knocked. Sally stood behind her, pensive.

'Terry?' She shot out past him into the street. 'Where's Keith? Sally said you went out to find him? Where is he!?' Katie screamed before breaking down in tears, heaving with the strain.

Sally took her in her arms and guided her back through to the front room. Watson closed the door behind him. Jason appeared at the top of the stairs. Terry told him to stay up there and to keep everyone busy.

Sally had sat Katie down on the leather settee. Watson entered and sat in one of the armchairs. Katie looked up at him and mouthed the words, 'Where is he? Is he dead?' Her voice barely audible. Watson sat forward and looked at his hands, clasped together in the gap between his knees. This was going to be tough to get through.

'Keith was signing off on some paperwork with our boss when I left HQ. Getting into his car to leave work he was attacked and bundled into a van by persons unknown to us at the moment. We are trying to track down the van. We have everybody on shift out looking throughout the city and beyond for him. Trust me we will not stop until he is found.'

Watson felt he was saying this not only to let Katie know but also to stop him from going nuts thinking of what his partner – not only on the job but in friendship – was going through. Was he in a ditch somewhere with a bullet in his head? And why?

Katie's sobs brought him back to the now. She just stared back at him. He could not tell if what he had just said had registered. Her eyes seemed vacant. The cogs in her brain were turning slowly trying to make sense of his words. A couple of times she looked like she was going to say something, mouth open, but nothing came out.

'Katie? Did you hear what I said?'

'Do you have any idea who took him or why?' Katie was slowly processing the situation.

'We don't know. There were no visible markings on the van and we could not see the number plate. I am speaking as a friend now, is there anything that you remember Keith saying to you or doing recently, something which you wondered about?' He knew he was clutching at straws.

'Like what?'

'I don't know. How has he been?'

'Normal I think, as far as normal goes with Keith.' Katie was still trying to get her head around it all. 'We had thrashed out the business with that bastard Jimmy Russell. Keith said he was done with the gambling business and would not go near it. As far as I know, he has not been near to that bloody casino. But we all know he has said that before.' Katie was close to tears again.

They looked at each other remembering his past lies which had almost wrecked the couple's marriage.

'Apart from the Russell business, how has he been at home?' Watson pressed.

Katie shrugged. 'He's been the dutiful husband. Home at normal times except when he is on a late duty with you. Took care of the kids. Oh my God, what am I going to tell them.' The tears started again as Katie hugged herself for comfort.

Sally rubbed Katie's shoulder and looked over at

Watson and shook her head.

'Please, Terry can we stop this for tonight? You need to get back to the office.' He nodded and said his goodbyes to Katie.

Sally followed him to the door. 'I will stay with her and ask mum to look after the kids for the night. Keep me updated by text. I will tell Katie anything she needs to know.'

They kissed and hugged before Watson left.

Sally quickly added, 'And while you are at it, go home and change, you smell of smoke.'

CHAPTER THREE

MONDAY EVENING/TUESDAY MORNING

DS Keith Monteith slowly came to. The floor beneath his body was cold and hard. His head felt like it had a hundred wild horses running through it. His body felt like he had gone one round with a heavyweight boxer. Had he broken a rib or two? Opening his eyes it was dark but by the smell of hessian and the rough fabric against his head he could tell he had a bag over it. He tried to move his hands which were tied behind his back. The cable ties cut into his wrists.

Wondering how he got here, he tried to focus his mind on anything he could remember. How long had he been here? Was he leaving work? Yes, that was it. He was walking out of the station to his car. Getting into his car? No, he didn't make it. Why? His memory was fuzzy. This bloody headache. At least he was alive. Was he attacked? Yes, but by who? He never saw them. Think!

His mind was a blank canvas as to what had happened after he'd been attacked. His frustration grew. He cursed under his breath. Not knowing if he was alone, or where he was. Listening, he tried to hear anything that would help him. Noises, talking, machinery, transport . . . There was nothing but silence.

'Help! Is anyone there?' He shouted twice, and immediately regretted it as the horses in his head came galloping through again. Shuffling his body around he tried to see if he could sit up against something. The hessian bag made it nearly impossible to see, so he lay on his back and rolled towards what he hoped would be one of the walls of the room he was in. After a few rolls, he banged into one, sending shockwaves through his already bruised and battered body.

His thoughts drifted to his family: wife of twelve years Katie and his daughters Rebecca and Pixie. What would they be doing now? Have they reported me missing? Is anyone looking for me? Whoever had taken him had removed his phone, car keys and wallet from his pockets, as he had not felt them as he'd rolled across the floor. His watch was also missing from his wrist.

Before he could work out how to get up off the floor, the decision was made for him. He heard the door being unlocked and opened. A bright light was switched on.

He was grabbed by the arms above the elbows and was dragged away from the wall and dumped onto what felt like a wooden chair.

'Take the bag off,' Someone barked. Monteith thought he recognised the voice, but couldn't be certain. The hessian bag was removed roughly off his head.

Monteith squinted slowly, opening his eyes to get them used to the full glaring light from the bulb overhead. When he stopped squinting, he could just make out his three abductors. Two he recognised as Jimmy Russell's goons Lex and Ray, from his previous visits to Russell's Casino. And the other belonged to the voice he recognised, Allan Russell, Jimmy's older brother.

'If this is how you treat all of your guests no wonder you're not on any of the travel sites,' Monteith said, trying to make light of the situation. He regretted his words as soon as he had spoken them however, when a punch to the stomach winded him.

Allan Russell walked over to Monteith and bent, face close. 'You are only still here and not in some ditch somewhere dead because of my brother. God only knows why!'

Allan stood back and gestured to Lex and Ray, 'Get our guest cleaned up, can't keep my brother waiting,' he said viciously.

Allan turned and left the room, slamming the door shut behind him, leaving Monteith staring at Lex and Ray and them at each other.

'Well, where's the shower then?' Monteith grinned at them. 'You heard him, can't keep the boss waiting.'

CHAPTER FOUR

TUESDAY MORNING

At 5 a.m. the CDA office looked like a dosshouse. There were police officers of all ranks using all the willpower they had to keep awake and to keep abreast of the situation, twelve hours in to the investigation. Coffee and tea mugs were littering the desks. As were the wrappers and bottles from various takeaways. The nightshift had come begun their duty, though some of the dayshift had refused to stop the search.

On the wall was a map of the city and surrounding areas, each of which were being crossed off as they were searched. There had yet to be a positive sighting of Monteith. Hotel receptionists, B&Bs, the railway station, and bus station were all given photos of Monteith and asked to report in if they had seen him.

In the room for the debrief by DCI Wright were Watson, Sgt Lorimer, and a couple of new arrivals: Detective Constables, Emma French, and Paul Sandall. A few uniformed officers had also joined them.

Gone was DCI Wright's pristine look she liked to keep. Smart clothes and tight neat hairdo. Now she was jacketless, blouse outside of her skirt, shoes off in stocking feet and hair untied and flowing.

Watson and Lorimer were in a worse state. After spending the majority of the evening and early morning on the lookout for their colleague and friend, they had collapsed in their chairs and slept for the last hour, physically and mentally drained. After a quick visit to the locker area for a face swill and toilet break, they were back awaiting the debrief. French and Sandall had been collecting all the information that came back from the search team. Both were still wired from all the coffee and energy drinks they had consumed.

Wright brought the debrief to order. 'Okay, almost twelve hours ago we had one of our own taken from beneath our noses, and we still don't know where he is.'

DC French began: 'We have covered the majority of the city. We're waiting to hear back from the teams from outlying villages. Divers have been into the weir because someone thought they had seen a body. Turned out to have been a mannequin dressed up.'

'Typical!' Lorimer grunted.

DC Sandall continued. 'We've searched what industrial units we could get into, both derelict and in use. Building sites and other disused buildings have all come up empty.'

'We did catch three lads breaking into the building site on St Peter's Street, and a van which was pulled over contained stolen goods which we may not have caught,' The Duty Sergeant added from the back of the room.

'Make sure you add them to your stats,' Lorimer said sarcastically.

'Piss off,' The Duty Sergeant snapped back. 'Don't forget you were one of us not so long ago.'

'Gentleman, leave the bickering out,' DCI Wright

cut in.

'Seriously, are we thinking now that someone has him tied up somewhere and he is unable to contact us?' Watson added to the mix, getting up from his chair to stretch his legs. 'I tried his phone numerous times. Went to voice mail at first, but since just after eleven o'clock last night it went dead. Probably out of battery.'

'So basically we have bugger all!' Wright said, frustratingly. 'Go and take a break and we will reconvene in an hour so we can set out what we need to do for the next shift changeover.'

-X-

On the other side of the city, Monteith, after being allowed to clean up, was being escorted by Jimmy Russell's thugs, Lex and Ray, from the vaults of the casino. The two looked like gorillas dressed in suits two sizes too small for them. They entered the main floor of the closed casino from the back. Cleaners were busy tidying up the mess from the night before. Nobody turned to watch the procession.

From the floor Monteith was taken by Lex and Ray through a private door and into a lift to the balconette where the offices were. Jimmy's was the biggest and the most opulent. Monteith had been there before, paying back his gambling debts with interest on top.

On entering Jimmy's office Monteith was forcibly seated onto a leather-backed chair facing Russell's large desk. Lex and Ray stood back from the chair but were easily in reach of Monteith in case he tried to make a move.

He looked around the office, taking in the grandeur of it all. He had not had the chance on his previous visits. The ornate wooden desk in front of him looked oriental in decoration, with Russell's computers and other things on it. A glass-fronted drinks cabinet sat in the corner behind the desk. There was a floor to ceiling bookcase, all matching the desk's oriental decoration. At the other end of the office was a three-piece dark green leather suite which was set around a large oval glass coffee table. The carpet plush, patterned. A large gold mounted mirror decorated with dragons on the wall by the door. Pictures of both the Russell brothers schmoozing with the great and good of West Ravenswood – councilors and company directors. Charity events and business gatherings at the best hotels. Everything a pair of crooks could want.

The main double doors to the office opened and the Russell brothers came in, deep in conversation, while looking at sheets of paper in a manila file.

Jimmy glanced over and smiled. 'Ah, Mr. Monteith! How are you?' Jimmy Russell asked, as he signed one of the sheets and gave the file back to his brother, before sitting down behind his desk. Allan stood back behind Jimmy.

'I'm okay, considering I have been abducted, beaten up, held a prisoner in the dark with my hands tied up with a concussion.' He wanted to sound sarcastic, but his anger at the treatment he'd received was on a scale of an erupting volcano.

Lex and Ray moved towards Monteith after his outburst, but a quick small shake of Jimmy's head sent them back to where they were standing. Another signal and they were ordered out of the office, leaving just Monteith and the Russell brothers alone with him.

'Well, I hope you will accept my apologies for your treatment. I only asked my boys to see if you would come and see me. If they were a bit over-enthusiastic, I will have a word with them.' Jimmy's smarminess was oozing out of every pore. Allan smirked. Jimmy continued, 'You see I've got a little proposition to put your way.'

'Could you not have just phoned me? And what makes you think I am interested in what you have to say? I have paid off my debt. End of story. I'll keep away from here if that's what you want.'

'No, on the contrary, I want you to come and work for me. As my Chief of Security,' Jimmy Russell said with a straight face.

Monteith let out a little laugh. 'What!?'
Both the Russell brothers just stared back at him.
'Why me? Why not Lex, Ray or someone else?'
'They're not family.'
'Nor am I.'

'Contrary to popular belief, I do like you and what you stand for,' Russell said from behind his ornate wooden desk. 'The others on my payroll like Lex and Ray just pay lip service. I say "jump" they say "how high?" I hear you have guts. You and your partner Watson.'

Russell got up from his chair and started pouring himself a drink from the cabinet.

Sitting back down, he continued. 'Come to work for me. You can do a lot better than you are doing now. What do you make as a detective? £30,000, £40,000. I can treble that. You could have anything you dream of. Just look around you. All the wealth and trappings. Do you really want to be Detective Plod of the police the whole of your life when you can be involved in all of this? I have big plans for the growth of this place.'

'Sell out to you?' Monteith replied. Unsure if what he had been offered was true or just a test.

'Sell out? No. Call it better job prospects. Will you get a promotion any time soon? Not with your background. I hear Matthews has already marked your cards.'

'And if I say no, I'm not interested in what you are offering?'

Jimmy and Allan exchanged glances. 'I could make life very difficult for you and your family.'

'You leave my family alone!' Monteith bellowed.

'Now there's the fire in you I like.' Jimmy Russell held his hands up in mock surrender. Getting up, he gestured to Monteith. 'Come with me. I have something to show you.'

He led Monteith out of his office and onto the balcony overlooking the casino floor.

'Take a look at that, a real look at what is before you.' Russell held his arms wide. Lines of fruit machines as far as you could see. Roulette tables, Poker tables. Blackjack, Baccarat. A long bar down one side sectioned off from the main floor. On the other side doors leading to a large restaurant.

Jimmy Russell continued. 'This is my dream. A dream I have had since I went into business. I want to expand this casino and I need someone who can advise me. I had to fire the last security officer for not doing his job properly.' Russell turned to face Monteith. 'I want you to take over. You will report to Allan.'

'Why don't you bring in a specialised security firm? Haven't you already taken one over?'

Monteith looked into Jimmy Russell's eyes. 'No. I like to keep security in-house and keep in tight. Hence why I had to let the previous incumbent go.'

Monteith considered asking what happened to him but thought better of it. 'I need time to think this over.'

'You've got to the end of the week or no deal and well . . .' Russell smiled, playfully tapping Monteith's cheek. 'Things could get tricky for you.' He signalled to Lex and Ray to escort Monteith downstairs.

Jimmy joined Allan back in his office. Allan was shaking his head.

'Hope you know what you are doing Jimmy.'

'I always know what I am doing.' Jimmy smiled before taking a swig of his drink.

'But are you sure he doesn't know?'

Jimmy turned to Allan. 'Friends close, enemies closer.'

CHAPTER FIVE

Dawn was slowly breaking over West Ravenswood. Night slowly turning into early morning. One squad car was trawling one of the industrial estates which had been searched earlier. Coming up to a roundabout they noticed something on it. It was propped up against one of the trees in its centre. They did a full circuit then pulled over.

'Looks like someone's playing silly buggers again,' PC Kendall said to his partner.

'Whatever it is, it's just moved. Look!' His partner pointed over as he was unclipping his seatbelt.

'Bet you it's a homeless person or a drunk,' Kendall said dismissively.

They both got out and approached what looked like a large bag of rags. As they got closer they could hear muffled groans.

'Come on you cannot sleep here on the roundabout it's not safe,' Kendall said to the human form slumped by his feet.

The bundle tried to speak but was incoherent.

'Hey, he's got a bag on his head. And his hands are tied.' His partner knelt down to pull it off.

'Just a minute fella, I will get it off . . . Bloody hell!'

Looking up at Kendall.
'I will radio it in. PC192 Kendall to base, over.'
'Base here, what's your status.'
'Base, we have just found DS Monteith.'

-X-

The ambulance arrived within minutes of the call and took Monteith to A&E to be checked over. He had complained of a severe headache and painful ribs. His wrists and ankles were cut by the tie wraps.

Wright, Watson, and Lorimer all rushed across to the hospital. After parking up, they flew into the reception area and on into the main department, leaving stunned receptionists and patients in their wake.

'Who the hell are you?' A disgruntled doctor bellowed at them, blocking their way.

DCI Wright waved her ID at the doctor. 'We're here to see DS Keith Monteith. He was brought in a few minutes ago. We need to speak to him.' She tried to look past the doctor to see where Monteith was, while inching forward towards A&E.

'I don't care if you are the Prime Minister. You don't come bursting in here. We are very busy with some very ill people. How dare you try and throw your weight around.' The doctor was joined by the duty manager for the department, who strongly objected to the way they had pushed themselves into her department and escorted them to a private waiting area. They were told in no uncertain terms to wait until a member of staff became available to update them.

CHAPTER SIX

TUESDAY 7 a.m.

The DCI ordered both Watson and Lorimer home for some rest while they were waiting for Monteith to be released from the hospital. They had all been working nonstop and were in serious need of a wash and some sleep. When Watson got back Sally had gone to work and the kids to school. Grabbing a mug of coffee before going upstairs, he stripped off and had a shower, getting rid the grime of a long and worrying night. True, Keith had been found but that was only just the start of it. The debrief would happen whenever he was released from the hospital, and they'd know who'd taken him.

Watson closed the curtains, set his alarm and lay back on the bed to drift off.

His dreams landed him back at the multi-storey car park prior to the shooting of the serial killer whose case he had only just completed. What could he have done to change the outcome? He was crouched down behind a car with his then boss DCI Kenneth Crompton. Their assailant was threatening to throw the two scroats who had murdered his wife from the top of the car park. The next thing he saw was Crompton shoot the man. Could he have stopped his boss before he pulled the trigger? And why had he done it?

Watson woke up in a sweat with the bed sheets all over the place. He sat up and wiped his damp brow with both his hands. Looking at the clock he had only been asleep for a couple of hours. He tried to lie down again but was too restless. An hour later, he put on some clean work clothes and went downstairs. Another coffee and two bacon baps were enough to give him the kickstart he needed. He had to return to the office before Jason, Simon and especially Rachael returned from school, or he would never get out. He loved his kids dearly and loved being with them, but work at this time came first. He left a note for Sally saying he would ring later.

Arriving at the station Watson had to manoeuvre his way through the press who had gathered outside. He parked his battered Ford Focus next to Monteith's. Ignoring the shouts for information, he got out and looked over at the BMW, 1 series. Still there was the dent in the roof made by Monteith during his mad rage after being given a grilling by Superintendent Matthews over his gambling.

'You are getting lax my friend in your pride and joy,' he said to himself, before entering the custody area.

'Any news on Keith?' The Duty Sergeant asked as he went by.

'Don't know. Just going to find out now, Bill. Will let you know later.' With that, Watson made for the stairs and up to the CDA Office.

The office was deserted. Watson went over to his desk and put his jacket over the back of his chair before booting up his computer. Something caught his eye in the boss's office as he glanced through the open door. A pair of stocking feet, which as he moved closer he realised belonged to his DCI. She was asleep in a chair with her feet on the coffee table. He smiled to himself as he looked at her from the door. Shapely legs disappearing under a knee-length black skirt. Jacket being used to cover up a clean white blouse. Hair hanging loosely around her face.

'Like what you see DS Watson?' DCI Wright said, opening an eye and grinning.

'Oh, sorry boss.' Watson smiled back. 'Didn't want to disturb you.'

'I heard you come in.' Wright slowly sat up, wincing.

'How long have you been here? Did you go home?' Watson asked.

'No, not been home. I stayed, in case we had an update from the hospital. I told the others to come back for four o'clock, What time is it now?'

'Ten to three. Come on I will treat you to something from the canteen.'

'You say the sweetest things, DS Watson,' Wright replied, laughing.

After a wash, Wright made her way up to the canteen.

Watson bagged them a table out of view of prying eyes.

'What are you going to do about Keith when he comes back?' Watson asked, as his boss sat opposite him tucking into a plate of scrambled eggs on toast.

'Depends how he is. Probably get him to take a few days off to recuperate while we search for his abductors. Any ideas on who it could be?'

Watson took a slurp from his cup. 'If he has got himself into something else since the gambling fiasco, I don't know if their marriage will survive this time.'

'How long has he been married to Katie?'

'Well, their eldest, Rebecca, is ten, so twelve years.'

Wright polished off the last bit of toast before asking, 'And you?'

'Me and Sally? Coming up for fourteen years this year.'

Wright nodded in thought and took a drink from her cup of tea. 'How long have you been a detective sergeant, Terry?'

Watson leaned back in his chair. His face creased as he tried to remember. 'Been at the CDA here for five years. Was made DS three years before, so eight in total. Why'd you ask?'

'Matthews is looking into bringing in a DI to the agency to oversee the operational side.'

'What? From outside the agency?' Watson was taken aback with what Matthews was suggesting.

'Yes. Unless I can think of anyone who fits the bill to act up.' Wright looked over her cup at Watson. Waiting to see how fast the lightbulb came on.

'Me!?' Watson almost fell back off his chair. 'Acting DI?'

Wright wiped her mouth with her serviette and pushed her plate to one side. 'Just a thought, Terry. You have been the longest here besides Monteith, and Matthews would never consider him for promotion. Lorimer is waiting to see if he has passed his detective's exam and the two others, French and Sandall, have only just arrived. Which leaves you. I can put your name forward. Have you thought about promotion before?'

'No, I've not. It's not crossed my mind.'

'Well think about it soon. I would like an answer before Matthews acts.'

CHAPTER SEVEN

TUESDAY 4 p.m.

The previous night's exploits had taken a lot out of everybody, both mentally and physically. Looking for a missing person is hard on those looking. Not knowing if they are alive or dead. Not knowing if you will see them again.

Lorimer, Sandall, and French were already in situ when Wright and Watson arrived back from the canteen shortly before the office doors opened and in walked Monteith.

'Did everyone miss me?'

'Bloody hell,' Lorimer exclaimed, as they all stood up and walked over to meet him.

'When were you released?' Wright asked, with concern written on her face.

'I discharged myself. Fed up with the missus moaning that I should get out of the service.'

'Where's Katie now?' Watson asked.

Monteith grinned 'Gone home in a taxi after dropping me off. I decided on the way home to come in to see you, much to her growing anger. She thought I was nuts coming in, never mind discharging myself. Only hope she's calmed down when I get back.'

They helped him across the office to his desk, as

he was still a little unsteady on his feet, probably from his head injury, 'Mind the ribs. Docs say I have cracked a couple,' Monteith said, trying not to laugh. He turned to Wright. 'You had better get Matthews down here. He may want to hear this.'

She looked at him, puzzled.

Minutes later Monteith was taking them through what had happened to him.

'I think there were two in the back with me. I could not tell how long we were in the van or SUV. We stopped a couple of times. Then I was dragged from the van and put into another vehicle. It felt more like a car that time. I felt carpet under me and it was cramped and dark. Just before I was put in the boot a bright flash blinded me for a couple of seconds, then it was gone. I must have blacked out after that because when I came to I was in a dark room.'

'We found a burned out van by the landfill. Sounds like you were in that,' Watson informed him.

Monteith then told them about his meeting with the Russells before he'd been dumped on the roundabout.

Wright turned to Superintendent Matthews who was sitting away from the group, 'That should be enough to raid and arrest the Russells for false imprisonment and ABH considering we've got the abduction on CCTV.'

'Yes, but they can say they knew nothing about what their henchmen had planned to do.'

'We cannot let them get away with what they have done to Terry,' Watson said.

'I understand your frustration, but let's just hang on,' Matthews commented.

He turned to Monteith. 'This is out of character behaviour for Allan Russell, which means whatever he wants you on the inside for is big.'

'But isn't this the chance we have been waiting for, to get on the inside of Russell's empire. He has opened the door so why don't we walk straight through?' Lorimer asked cautiously.

Matthews stood looking out of the office window, the cogs in his mind whirring round. 'When does Allan want your answer?'

'End of the week,' Monteith replied with a little concern in his voice.

Matthews turned and made eye contact with Monteith. 'Would you be willing to take up his offer, and report back to me what they're up to?'

'He's invited his own mole into his hole.'

'I'll take that as a "yes" then shall I?'

He nodded.

'DCI Wright and I will work out a scenario for you to start working for Russell and make it as if you have left the agency.'

'I don't like it, sending Terry into the Russells is tantamount to signing his death warrant,' Watson voiced with concern.

'You can be his handler. If Terry gets in trouble we will pull him out,' Wright assured Watson.

Monteith and Watson looked at each other and speaking at the same time said, 'Agreed.'

CHAPTER EIGHT

TWO WEEKS LATER – MONDAY 8.30 a.m.

'Right, Mum, I'm off.' Alison Grant called up the stairs of their three-bed semi situated in the Normanton part of West Ravenswood. She was dressed in her running gear with her long brown hair tied back in a ponytail.

Her mother, Joan, leaned over the banister at the top of the stairs with a shirt hanger in her hand. 'Are you doing your short run or long run this morning darling?'

'Short run today – should be back in an hour.' Alison stood on the bottom step so her mother could see her. Joan Grant started down the stairs. 'Your Aunty Debbie would be so proud of you if she was still alive.'

'I know, Mum. That's why I'm running the city's half marathon.' Alison hugged her Mum tightly. Both of them had tears in their eyes.

'Okay, stay safe.' Joan smiled at her daughter, saying what she always said before anyone from the family left the house.

'Always do, Mum. I need to go as Marcus will be round later and we are going into town.' Alison had with her a small bottle of water. She put in her earphones which were connected to her phone where she had her training music, started the stopwatch on her wrist and shut the front door behind her.

'Why do they have to grow up so fast?' Joan said to herself, as she looked at her reflection in the hall mirror before giving it a wipe with the duster.

Alison had been sporty from an early age. She played tennis and was always running around with bundles of energy. The sports teacher at Saint Mary's Academy, Stuart Wilkins, quickly introduced her to the athletics team. She became a star at 800 metres and the cross-country, winning or coming second in all her races against the other schools in the city and surrounding areas. This brought her to the attention of the local athletics club and she began training with Ian Fellows, who guided her on how to make the most of her burgeoning talent.

Alison's auntie Debbie passed away from breast cancer six months ago, so she decided to run the local half-marathon to raise money for breast cancer research. Training most days, she increased the length of her runs until she could easily clock around two hours.

Alison set out from her home and took the path in between two of the neighbouring houses, which led to an unmanned crossing over the railway tracks, and out over to the countryside at the back of her house. She was careful to look both ways along the two-track railway. The locals had tried to get a bridge built over the tracks, but it was turned down as the frequency of the trains was minimal it would be a waste of money, or so the council said.

On the other side of the crossing the path came out on to the end of a country lane. It used to be longer, but when the railway was laid in the 1960s and the housing estate was built in the 1980s, it was reduced in length. Railway workers now used it to park their vans when there was maintenance work to be done on the branch line. Also, to the annoyance of the locals, it was used as a dumping ground by fly-tippers.

Alison, with her music playing and concentrating on her running, was oblivious to the blue van which was parked there today with its bonnet open. The only thing she remembered was the sharp pain at the back of her head. And then her legs buckle from underneath her, as she hit the stone chipped road with a sickening thump. Everything went fuzzy and blurry as her mouth filled with the metallic taste of blood.

CHAPTER NINE

An old grey trainer that had once been white was stuck deep in the hedge about half way up. The red streaks of plastic on its side were faded with the moisture which had got inside them. The laces were frayed at the end after losing their aglet plastic coating. How it got there nobody knew. It had been there for some months, and where was the other one? The grass and stinging nettles underneath were so thick you had trouble seeing anything in there.

The hedge was part of the border which separated a local farmer's field and industrial wasteland to the south of West Ravenswood. The industry had come and gone in a short period, leaving the land and buildings to nature. Burned out cars and vans, fridges, fridge-freezers, beds and three-piece suites of all sizes had been tossed onto the site. The kids used the mounds of earth and rubbish as a makeshift playground. BMX tracks and jumps were made. Stolen cars were driven around by underage drivers before they were set on fire. But over the last month workers had begun to clear the land, bought by a local property developer, ready for the building of a new housing estate. But the clearance had now been stopped.

DI Terry Watson showed his badge to the uniformed officer on the gates of the industrial estate and parked his Ford Focus next to the portacabin office. Getting out, he noticed a group of workers in safety helmets, boots, and fluorescent jackets gathered around the tea wagon. The smell of bacon, eggs, sausages and fried onions cooking hit Watson's nostrils at full force. The tea and toast he'd had for breakfast was not filling enough. He would make a point of stopping there on his way out.

Watson asked one of the workers where he could find the project manager and was directed to a double portacabin. One situated on top of the other. As he climbed the metal stairs to the top one he could hear a raised voice through the open door.

'How the hell do I know . . .? I've not been told . . . They've kept us away from the area . . . Some DI from the police is supposed to be coming . . . Let you know later . . .'

The stout looking man slammed the phone down and turned the air blue with swear words even Watson had never heard before. Watson knocked on the open door.

'Who the hell are you?'

'I'm the DI you are waiting for.'

'Shit.' The man stood, mouth open for a second before regaining his composure. 'Sorry, you had to hear that. Pressure from the powers above to get this thing moving – pain in the ass they are. They should come down and do a day's proper work. We're already behind, and now this.'

The man shuffled sideways through the gap between his desk and the office wall and held his large hand out. 'Ray Wilson.'

'DI Terry Watson. What happened this morning?'

Both men moved out onto the metal stairs. The view of the industrial estate was below and to their left, spanning a good couple of acres. A large industrial unit towered in the centre of the area. Police tape had been put up all the way around it. Two uniformed officers were at the large front door. The forensics team was already there, dressed in their white overalls and face masks. Watson spotted the pathologist James MacIntosh's van parked close by.

'Some of the lads were in there cleaning it out before we pulled it down. It was once used as a garage and MOT place. We were trying to dig out and remove the ramps and brake testers. One of the ramps looked quite new. As we removed it a large chunk of cement from the floor came with it. A lad spotted carpet in the hole. He pulled at it and the body was underneath it. That's when we called you . . .'

One of the portaloos opened as they were talking. A skinny lad no more than nineteen years old came out.

'That's the lad who found it, Paul. He's been puking his guts up ever since.'

'You never forget the first time you see a dead person,' Watson said with some sympathy, looking down at the lad as he turned and bolted for the loo again. 'Right, I had better see the crime scene. Thanks, Mr Wilson.' Watson started down the stairs to his car.

'I will take you over in my van if you don't mind. I need to get an update myself on how long this is going to take. Also, it will give my ears a rest from the boss's telephone calls.' Ray Wilson locked the office and followed Watson down to the car park and directed him to a white Nissan Navarra.

'You will need this as well.' Wilson lobbed a safety helmet to Watson as they got in.

The drive over was quick and Ray Wilson parked up next to the police tape. He got out but Watson stopped him from going any further.

'As this is a crime scene you will have to remain here,' Watson reminded him.

'But I need to find out when we can get back to work. My neck's on the line here!'

'I understand, but I cannot let you in. Look, I will have a word with forensics. That's all I can do.' Watson dipped under the tape heading for the building, leaving a frustrated Wilson kicking the tyre of his van. 'Keep an eye on him will you,' Watson whispered to the constable guarding the main door. The constable nodded and stood a little more alert than he had been.

Watson signed in to show he had attended, donned a pair of shoe covers, gloves, face mask and safety helmet, before making his way over to the far corner where a forensics tent stood. He thought back to what he said about seeing your first dead person and never forgetting it. He could remember *all* the dead people he had seen.

James MacIntosh appeared from out of the tent, stretching his back.

'Having fun in there, Mac?' Watson joked as he made his way across to him.

Mac removed his mask, trying to gulp in some fresh air. 'Hi there stranger, wondering if you'd be turning up for this one.' The stench of rotting flesh filled the air.

'You got a new aftershave Mac?'

'You noticed. It's called Corpse. The essence of decomposition mixed with bloated gas and a smidgen of dead fly larvae. Does wonders for your love life.'

'Didn't know you had one?' Watson said smiling.

'I don't!' Mac laughed.

'What do we have in your tent of wonders?'

'Let me show you. You'll need to hold your breath though.' Mac opened the tent flap and they both entered.

'It's not as bad as the time we fished that bloated body out of the river.'

Mac laughed. 'No that was really terrible. This is just a six on the gagging scale.'

An eight by six foot hole had been dug around the carpeted and tied up body.

'We have taken the normal pictures during the excavation to catalogue the evidence while the body was still in situ. Anything of interest found we bagged and tagged,' Mac continued. 'We are close to bringing the body out of there.'

'Female or male?'

'Don't know, to look at what was left of the face. With a couple of hundredweight of concrete poured onto it, they are not looking their best at the moment. Will be able to give you a proper rundown of age and how they died and approximate time of death when we get back to do the autopsy.'

Mac turned to his partner. 'I think we can prepare to slowly try and remove now.'

Both Watson and Mac came back out of the tent, taking off their gloves and masks, slowly walking towards the main door. Mac broke the silence.

'Have you heard from Keith recently?'

Watson looked into the distance. 'No, not since he resigned.'

'It surprised me, him doing that. I thought you two were as thick as thieves, excuse the pun?'

Watson struggled with talking about his best friend. 'He had some personal troubles during the

Freeman case. Old skeletons from his past came back to haunt him. I think it just took too much out of him. He needed to get away from everything.'

'I heard his Mrs divorced him and took the kids?'

'I know she has moved out of the house with the kids, but divorce I cannot say.'

Ray Wilson spotted Watson.

'When am I getting my site back?' he shouted.

'Who's that guy?' Mac asked, as he unlocked his van.

'The site manager. He's getting hassle from his bosses over this. Not being able to work. He needs to know when you will be finished so they can get on.'

'Tell him not for the rest of the day at least.'

'I have to get back. Let us know when you are starting the autopsy.' Watson shook hands with Mac and turned towards where Ray Wilson was standing.

Wilson went scarlet with rage when Watson told him what Mac had said when they drove back to the main office.

They parked up. Wilson stormed up the metal stairs to his office, slamming the door, not giving Watson a second glance. The smell from the tea wagon was overpowering. Grabbing a bacon and egg bap covered with tomato sauce and a tea, Watson settled in his car. As he took a mouthful his phone went off. Noticing it was Wright, he quickly swallowed his mouthful of bap and answered.

'Morning, boss.'

'Where are you, Terry?' The DCI sounded worried.

'I'm down at the Copeland Industrial Estate. Got a call a body had been found. Did nobody tell you?'

'Yes, I was just checking if you were going to be back for the morning debrief. We have a lot to catch up on.'

'I just have something to finish off first. I will be in

by 10 a.m.'

'You take your time with your breakfast, don't mind us.'

Watson looked at his phone in disbelief as the DCI clicked off. Then down at his tie which had tomato sauce down it. 'Shit'.

CHAPTER TEN

MONDAY 10 a.m.

The office of the Criminal Detective Agency erupted in laughter and cheers when Watson walked in.

'Where's ours, you tight bugger?' Sergeant Lorimer shouted, as he brought a large file back to his desk.

'Back at the tea bar, you still owe me for the one last week,' Watson shot back as he put his stuff down on his desk and took off his jacket.

'Bollocks, I paid you for that one.' Lorimer stood pointing his finger at Watson.

'When you two have finished we have some work to go through.' DCI Wright had come out of her office and was standing by the list of ongoing cases on the board.

'Now before I start, Karl will you come to the front please.'

'What? Boss, we were only joking. I will pay Terry back, honestly.' Lorimer looked alarmed. 'Here Terry, here's a tenner.' He threw a folded note on Watson's desk.

'Well, you won't want what I have for you, Detective Sergeant Lorimer.' DCI Wright stood holding a brand new ID card. 'I have just heard you have passed your DS exam, and with all the good work you have been doing since I have been here, I hope you will stay on with the agency.

The room again erupted, this time in cheers and whoops. A lot of back-slapping, and congratulations for Lorimer, as he shook hands with everyone. The last being DCI Wright, as she hooked the lanyard containing his new card round his neck.

'Right then, simmer down. Let's get on. Terry, can you start off with this morning's call?' Wright asked.

'Got called out to Copeland Industrial Estate where a body was found by workmen demolishing the industrial units. It was buried under the concrete floor of the last remaining unit. The place had previously been used as a garage and MOT service centre. Mac was there when I turned up but had not removed the body from the hole. An autopsy will probably be tomorrow at the earliest.'

'Isn't that where they are going to build that new housing estate?' Paul Sandall asked, when Watson had finished. 'Looked very plush from the drawings and sketches I have seen.'

'Yes. I spoke to a very frustrated site manager, Ray Wilson. He was getting an ear-bashing from the new owners who want the work to commence ASAP. He was not thrilled when we told him he might not get his site back until tomorrow, if he's lucky.'

The DCI turned to Lorimer. 'Right, DS Lorimer, what are you working on?'

'Debit card fraud.'

'Don't get caught now you're a DS.'

'As I was saying,' Lorimer started again. 'A group of fraudsters is targeting the town centre buying small priced items, under the £100 limit before you have to put your pin number in to confirm. They have been hitting supermarkets, games shops, and entertainment stores. We are waiting for the stores involved to give up their CCTV coverage.'

'If you need any help on that, DC French can join you in looking through the images,' Wright added. French nodded and looked over at Lorimer.

'DS Sandall, you've been on these burglaries?'

'Yes, distraction burglaries. There have been four over the last week that we know of. We are getting the victims in to do photofits of the men involved. We can get pictures out to the press within an hour of completion.'

'Right, let's get on then. Terry, can you join me, please?' DCI Wright signalled for Watson to follow her into her office. She had already sat down behind her desk when he was near entering.

'Can you shut the door behind you please?'

Watson did as he was asked and sat down on the chair in front of Wright's desk which faced the window with a view of the city.

'I just wanted a chat to see how you are.' Wright leaned back in her chair and looked at Watson.

Watson rubbed an imaginary hair from his trousers.

'You haven't been going to see the counsellor recently have you?'

Watson looked as if he was going to say something but Wright put her hand up to stop him.

'I've been checking because you're a valuable and experienced member of this team.'

'It's not working for me, all this talking about my feelings.'

'After what happened in your previous case and to my predecessor . . . things like that leave a stain.'

'Is that speaking from experience?' Watson queried.

'We are talking about you, not me.' Wright looked

uneasy, getting out of her chair and pouring a glass of water. Still with her back to Watson, she asked, 'How are you sleeping? You've seemed not to be with it sometimes?'

'Not brilliant, still getting flashbacks to the car park, wondering if I could have prevented it.'

'Don't punish yourself.' Wright turned back to Watson. 'From what I have been told by others, and reading all the reports, you did all you could. Nothing was going to stop Crompton from shooting Littlewood. He had made his own mind up. What was left of it! If you or anyone else had got in the way that day you would not be here sitting in front of me.' Wright was trying to talk to Watson more as a work colleague than as a boss, using a calm and measured voice, but Watson was not having any of it.

'Try telling that to my brain at 3 a.m,' Watson fired back.

Sitting on the edge of her desk, Wright said, 'That's what the counsellor is for Terry. Go and see him, please.'

'Is that all boss?' Watson leaped up.

'Yes, that's all,' Wright sighed.

As they came out of the office, Lorimer was deep in conversation on his phone.

'Boss, we have a missing person,' Lorimer got out of his chair and showed the details to DCI Wright.

'Can't uniform deal with it?' French asked, as she swivelled around from her desk. 'We have enough on our plate as it is.'

'Not this one, A seventeen year old female, Alison Grant, went for her normal morning run at about 8 a.m. and has not returned. Said she would be an hour and now it's 11.30 a.m. Family and her boyfriend have been looking along the route she always takes and there is no sign of her.'

'How about friends?' Sandall queried. 'Did she stop off at someone's?'

'The family have spoken to them and none of them have seen her. Besides, they don't live on the route,' Lorimer replied.

Wright scanned over the details on the paper. 'Okay, Watson, can you take DC French with you and interview the family. Get as much information on the young woman as you can. I will arrange for a family liaison officer to join you.'

CHAPTER ELEVEN

The blue van pulled into the driveway of the farmhouse. The countryside around the east side of West Ravenswood was flat and inhospitable. Houses were sparse; with most neighbours so far away you needed binoculars just to see them.

The driver got out of the van, checking his passenger was still with him, before making his way to the house, unlocking the front door. He was carrying his work bag and a tool bag. He put his tool bag by the front door and switched on the hall light, before carrying the bag with him into the kitchen.

He had lived on his own for a couple of years. The farmhouse had belonged to his parents before they had passed away. He'd not married, spending some of his time helping out on the farm and the rest setting up his joinery and fencing business. He rarely ventured into West Ravenswood. The house and one small warehouse were all that was left after he had sold off the land to the adjoining farmers.

After having had a drink he went back out to the van, unlocking the back doors. Inside, on a mattress was his passenger. Picking her up he carried her over his shoulder back into the house. Her legs were tied around the ankles and her wrists were tied behind her back. Her mouth was covered in tape. Opening the wooden door under the stairs, putting the light on, he went down the ten steps carefully. At the bottom, there was a hallway with pictures on the walls. Two bare light bulbs hung from the ceiling, one at each end of the hallway. At the far end was a padlocked door. Pulling the key out of his pocket, he opened it to reveal a small room.

He slowly and carefully laid the young woman down on another mattress. She was still unconscious, her hair damp and sticky with blood. Her face and hands were covered in cuts after her fall onto the road. The knees of her tracksuit were torn.

Taking out the old Nikon camera he stood beside her and started snapping photos of her. When he'd finished, he knelt down and cut off a few strands of hair from her head. Standing, he made his way to the other end of the room. Three shelves had been erected on the wall, each with small plastic see-through boxes on it. Matchbox in size, each contained human hair. He removed an empty box and placed the young woman's into it. Marking it with a name and date, he added it to his collection.

CHAPTER TWELVE

Monteith begrudgingly opened his eyes. He was flat out on his stomach on his bed, still fully clothed. The bedside light was still on even though it was now daylight. Moving the half-drunk can of beer away from the bedside clock he glanced at it, 12.30 p.m. Sitting up, Monteith switched the bedside light off only to find that the hall light had also been left on. He remembered getting in at about 4 a.m. from the casino, but that was it.

He stripped off his well-worn and slept in clothes and stepped into the shower. Twenty minutes later he was washed, changed and downstairs. In the front room, there were remnants of a Chinese takeaway on the table with another two beers. When he had had that, Monteith could not remember.

In the kitchen, he switched on the local radio station while he cleaned the remnants of the takeaway and beer cans away. The news was reporting about a girl who had gone missing, a gang of fraudsters in the city and something about burglaries. Listening to it, he thought he should be back in the thick of it dealing with the bread and butter of the agency. He also thought back to the dressing down he had been given from Superintendent Matthews, and why he did not tell him to stick this undercover lark where the sun doesn't shine. He might have been better off out of the force, doing things he wanted to do. Instead, he was risking his life trying to get information against the biggest and most dangerous crook in the city, Jimmy Russell.

The days were merging into one another.

The house was also too quiet. His wife had taken the girls to her mothers and was threatening divorce if he did not stop this undercover assignment. She wanted her old husband back and not this knackered old shell of a man he had become. But now, two weeks later, here he was, according to the Aerosmith song F.I.N.E.: Fucked Up, Insecure, Neurotic and Emotional.

CHAPTER THIRTEEN

Watson and DC French pulled into the road where Grant's house was. They parked behind the police car which had been sent to the address after the initial report of the missing young woman had been made. From where they were, they could see through the front bay window. The place looked to be in chaos. There appeared to be an increasingly animated argument taking place between a man and women, with a couple of teenagers standing by, attempting to get their words in, while fingers were being pointed.

DC French went to get out. Watson put a hand on her arm.

'Hang on!' he said quietly. 'Let's just see how this plays out.' He nodded towards the house. French looked quizzical.

'Normally I would go straight in, but it looks like there is something of a blame game ongoing. Trust me, you don't want to get caught up in that.'

A Police Constable exited his car and jumped into the back of Watson's.

'How long has this been going on, constable?' Watson looked back at the officer through the rearview mirror.

'PC Gary Kendal, sir. About five minutes, as soon as the man arrived. That's his car on the driveway, the silver Mercedes. I was inside talking to the mother, Joan Grant, when he turned up.'

'I take it he's the husband?' French asked.

'Yes. David Grant. He was not happy and told me to leave, having asked me why I was not out looking for his daughter.'

'A charmer then!,' French snorted her distaste.

'Who else is in there?' Watson asked, while keeping his eyes on the house.

'Their son, Alex, and Alison's boyfriend Marcus Devonport,' Kendal read from his notes.

'Well, I think it's time to meet the happy family, don't you?' Watson commented, as he started to get out of the car.

The three of them walked up the drive to the front door, glancing inside the Merc. Titanium briefcase left on the back seat with a copy of today's *Times*. Hands-free cradle for the phone and satnav perfectly placed for ease of use. Before they reached the door, it was opened by Joan Grant. Tears were streaming down her cheeks as she tried to force a smile of welcome.

'Have you found her?' Joan asked, with a gulp of air punctuating each word.

'I haven't heard mention yet and I'd be first to know. I'm DI Watson. These are my colleagues; DC French and you have met PC Kendal.' They each showed her their ID cards. 'Are you up to answering some questions?'

Joan Grant nodded and held the door open for them.

In the living room, introductions were gone through and everyone settled down. Apart from David Grant, who stood by the French windows looking out on to the back garden. He was simmering with what looked like rage. He had only grunted when Watson had introduced himself.

Watson started. 'Mrs Grant, can you tell us what happened this morning?'

David Grant butted in angrily. 'Our daughter went missing. Why are you questioning us when you should be out there looking for her?' He turned to face the room, face red. Which could have been caused by the drink he had been knocking back since he had arrived.

'David, please,' Joan snapped. 'Sorry, Detective Watson, My husband thinks he can order everyone around like he does at work. Alison said goodbye to me at about 8.30. She said she was doing her short run which usually takes her about an hour. She's training for the city's half marathon. Running it for breast cancer. By eleven o'clock she was not back. When Marcus, her boyfriend arrived, he went looking for her, while I rang her friends just in case she met someone. Marcus came back alone, so we rang the police.' Joan Grant broke down and sobbed. Her son Alex sat down beside her, while David Grant remained standing. Watson made a mental note of his inaction.

Watson turned to Marcus who was standing by the front window.

'How often does she go running, Marcus?'

'About four times a week now,' Marcus explained, while looking at his phone as if willing her to ring it.

Joan glanced at her husband through her tears.

'Have you called her phone?' Watson asked.

'Yes, but it just rings out then goes to voicemail. Alison uses it to listen to music when she runs.'

Watson and French exchanged glances. 'Do you have a recent photo of Alison that we can use? Does she use Facebook or other social media?'

'I have some on my phone you can use.' Marcus started flicking through his pictures. 'I took a couple last night when we were in town.' He leaned over to show DS French.

'Can you send them to my email address please?' French gave Marcus her card. He started tapping away on his phone before exclaiming, 'Done.'

There was a sharp knock on the front door. Watson asked Kendal to answer it. He re-entered with a female police officer. Watson stood up.

'Ah, PC Sharon Walsh, our family liaison officer. She will be staying with you. Any information we, or you, have, PC Walsh will act as a go-between.

David Grant swung round from where he was standing to face the room, glass of whiskey still in his hand, 'Why? So you can spy on us. Do you believe we have something to hide?'

'No, Mr Grant, that's not why PC Walsh will be here. She is here to help you. If you can remember something that might help in finding your daughter, PC Walsh can inform us. And if we need to pass anything on to you, it will come via her, and much faster than us having to call or someone round every time we have an update.' Watson looked at David Grant and the glass. 'I trust you will not be driving for the rest of the day?'

'Thank you, detective inspector,' Joan Grant butted in, glaring at her husband. 'Any help you can give in finding Alison is most appreciated.' She held out her hand. 'Sharon is it? Welcome. Do you want a drink?'

'May I have a look at Alison's room please?'

'Why?' Joan asked, confused. David Grant swung round wanting to say something, but stopped himself.

'I have been asked to collect something which has Alison's DNA on it, like a hairbrush or toothbrush. It's so we have something on record if we get a lead on where she is. Also, I need to take swabs from all the family.'

This was always the hardest thing to ask a parent to hand over, and Sharon could never get used to doing it.

'David Grant couldn't hold back, 'So you are saying we got rid of our own daughter.'

Watson walked over, 'I suggest you keep your thoughts to yourself and let PC Walsh do what she came here to do, or I could arrest you now for obstructing an ongoing police investigation.'

Joan took Sharon through the living room and up the stairs. On the landing, she pointed to Alison's room.

Sharon opened the door. It was not a typical girl's room, Alison was more of a tomboy. On one of the walls she had posters of Paula Radcliffe, Jo Pavey, and Lisa Dobriskey. Tracksuits were hung on the outside of her wardrobe. She noticed a couple of framed photographs of Marcus, one on his own in the park, the other was of both of them in an embrace.

On the dressing table, Sharon found a hairbrush. Putting on gloves she put the brush into an evidence bag and wrote the time, date, and from who and where it came from onto the front. Joan showed her which toothbrush was Alison's, which Sharon also bagged and tagged.

Coming back out of the room she nodded to Joan. 'Thank you.'

Watson realised they had outstayed their welcome and signaled his intention to leave for Kendal and French. 'I think we'll be off.' He said to anyone listening. Passing Marcus, he leaned in, 'Marcus; can I see you outside?'

Gathering by the cars, Marcus made another call to Alison's phone which went straight to voicemail.

'Mrs Grant said you went along the route Alison did for her short run?' DC French asked Marcus when he came off the phone.

'She went out on to the country lanes via the cut-through over there. It leads over the railway.'

He ordered a couple of squad cars to come down and search the route.

'How long have you been seeing Alison?'

'We have been together for about eighteen months. Met at school.'

'Has there been any trouble at home that you know of?'

Marcus shook his head. 'No, none that Alison told me of. Her dad can be a pain as you saw, but if you think he's done something to Alison then sorry, no.'

'So she wouldn't have just taken off of her own accord?'

'No, she would have told me, and if she had thoughts of leaving home I would have tried to talk her out of it.'

Kendal's radio sprung into life asking for help at an RTA nearby. 'Sorry, I have to take this.'

'No worries, we have finished here,' Watson told him. 'You get off. Thank you for your help.'

French stared out at the city landscape as they made their way back to HQ. She glanced at Watson who was concentrating on the traffic building up around the Rhubarb bridge roundabout.

'Well, what do you think of that?' French asked.

'Something's not right. There is more to this than they are letting on.'

'Hopefully Sharon can get the trust of Joan Grant. Don't think we can get much out of David.'

Watson signalled while switching lanes. 'Marcus may be a weak link. I think another interview with him away from the family may help. When we get back we need to put out a bulletin on Alison's disappearance. Contact the media. She may be in a ditch somewhere injured.'

Watson's phone on the dashboard cradle started to beep. He glanced at the screen and pressed a couple of buttons.

'Anybody want us?' French asked.

'No, just cold callers.'

Back at headquarters, Watson and French brought DCI Wright up to date with their visit to the Grant's. They arranged for a sweep of the area Alison used to reach the route she took, and French passed the photos of Alison that Marcus had sent to them on to the local media.

'What do you think?' Wright was talking to Watson while they were refilling their cups.

'I don't know. But I like the family for withholding something from us.'

'How did they seem while you were there?' Wright asked as they came back to their desks.

'Marcus, the boyfriend, was keeping a low profile, though was acting helpful when I spoke to him. The father, on the other hand, was trying to throw his weight around. He had been called back from work and I don't think he appreciated it, even if his daughter had gone missing. He was drinking too – heavily.'

'What kind of work does he do?'

'He owns a company. That's all I know.'

As Wright left, Watson keyed David Grant's name into the search bar of the Companies House website. He got 14,000 hits. He released a huff.

Taking his phone out, he texted Sharon Walsh.

> What does David do for a living?

CHAPTER FOURTEEN

Watson parked his Ford Focus outside the Royal Oak in South Meadows. Getting out he glanced around at the other cars, spotting the one he was looking for. With it being lunchtime the car park was almost full.

Entering through the door, he casually surveyed the clientele before approaching the bar. It prided itself in being one of the traditional public houses in the area, which had not given over to a modern chain-based choice of décor. No large flatscreen TV on the wall displaying a sports channel. No food from the same menu as a dozen or so other pubs. Even the drinks were locally brewed.

After ordering half a pint of bitter he asked for the lunchtime menu, homemade dishes using fresh food from local markets. He walked from the bar over to the restraurant where the pub menus graced the tables, found somewhere to sit and waited for someone to come and take his order.

'Thought you wouldn't turn up?' Monteith, who was already seated, said, sipping his pint.

'Busy morning,' Watson replied as he sat down.

'I heard on the radio before I left. Missing young woman; body found buried and the usual nutters trying to ruin things for the rest of us.'

'All in a day's work, you should know that. Or have you lost your mojo since leaving?' Watson commented, while glancing at the menu.

'I wish I was still doing it instead of looking at banks of screens every night, thanks to Matthews and the Russells.' Monteith started pulling apart a beer mat. 'Has some fringe benefits though. Some nice ladies I can look at every night. Look, but don't touch.' Monteith raised his eyebrows and grinned.

Watson tried to stifle a laugh but failed. 'Typical!'

'Well looking at them is better than looking at the bald and flabby men or the flash kids losing their money faster than a Lewis Hamilton lap record around Silverstone. I've been there and got a lot of T-shirts, remember?'

One of the restaurant staff, who looked like she should still have been in school, wandered over to see if they were ready to order. Watson asked for a BLT baguette with salad. Monteith ordered the same, with chips.

'How are the bands of brothers?' Watson asked after the waiter had moved on.

'Keeping their powder dry, at the moment. Nothing stands out for us to grab hold of. They are behaving themselves or keeping things quiet until they decide I'm not a threat. Their last Chief of security, the one who left suddenly, his name's Tommy Burke. Lex one of Jimmy's bodyguard's told me.'

'I'll check him out and get back to you,' Watson said.

As they made their way into the car park, Watson's phone dinged with a text message. He looked pleased with what he had received.

'Sally sending you dirty texts again,' Monteith

laughed, while trying to locate his car keys.

'I wish,' Watson replied. 'No, that was the family liaison officer who is taking care of the missing girl's parents. She's just given me the name of the firm the dad, David Grant, works for: Argent Logistics.'

'Argent Logistics?' Monteith asked.

Yes, you heard of them?'

'I saw Allan carrying a file into Jimmy's office the other day with that name on it.'

CHAPTER FIFTEEN

TUESDAY MORNING 3.23 a.m.

Where was he? Back at the multi-storey?,Why? He was still crouched down behind a car with DCI Crompton. Crompton moved, standing up and shooting Littlewood. Where had his boss got his gun?
'No stop, don't shoot!'

-X-

'Terry, Terry wake up.' Sally was shaking him.
'What!?' Watson shot up.
'It's okay darling. You were shouting.' Sally was sat beside him, stroking his head and back. 'You were having that nightmare again.'
Watson looked around the dark bedroom, lit only by the street lamp. He wiped the sweat from his face. 'Yes.' He threw the bedclothes back and peeled himself off the sodden sheet, swilling his face with cold water in the bathroom.
Sally followed him. 'Anything I can do to help?' Sally asked as she put her arms around him from behind. Watson dried his face and turned to face her, still in her embrace, kissing her on the lips.
'Thank you, but no. I have to work this out for

myself.'

'Have you made that appointment with the counsellor?' Sally said, looking up at him.

'Don't you start!' Watson broke away from his wife. 'The boss was on about seeing the head doctor yesterday morning.' Watson padded across the landing back to their bedroom.

Sally quickly checked on Rachael as she was passing before following.

'And she is right. Counselling could help you. At least think about it,' Sally said, getting back into bed with her husband.

Watson laid back with his arm covering his eyes, hoping to block the night out. Not wanting to fall asleep again.

Sally moved across and lay with her face on his chest. 'For me, and the kids?'

'I'll think about it.'

CHAPTER SIXTEEN

TUESDAY 9 a.m.

Watson pulled into the only parking space available behind the West Ravenswood Hospital. He managed to get back to sleep after the nightmare but kept on tossing and turning till the alarm went off. Hence he was not feeling brilliant this morning.

James MacIntosh, the pathologist, had rung late the previous afternoon to say that he was going to do the autopsy on the body in the carpet found at Copeland Industrial Estate. DCI Wright agreed that Watson should be present.

Walking into the morgue, Mac's signature music hit Watson's eardrums as soon as he opened the door. AC/DC's Dirty Deeds Done Dirt Cheap ramped up full blast. Mac was getting his tools of the trade ready when he looked up and saw Watson. He turned the music down allowing a proper conversation to take place.

'You must have titanium eardrums,' Watson joked.

'Heavy Metal must be played loud.'

'It's okay in a large venue or an outdoor festival, but in here? Jesus, it's enough to give you brain damage, never mind hearing loss.'

'Did you know that on July 15, 2009, in Canada,

Kiss achieved a 136 decibels during their live performance? After noise complaints from neighbours in the area, the band was forced to turn the volume down.'

'Judging from the noise I heard coming in here it's a wonder some of your guests don't complain, and they're dead.'

Both burst out laughing until Mac's assistant entered the mortuary.

Mac directed Watson to the vantage room overlooking the morgue.

'You can ask questions through the intercom as we go along.'

For the next two hours, Mac and his assistant slowly peeled back the carpet and black sheeting covering the body, being careful not to lose anything of significance and recording everything that they did by taking pictures and audio reporting their findings. Watson kept his questions to a minimum as he watched Mac work.

Now he knew the body was that of a female, aged approximately twenty-five to thirty years old. She was five foot, seven inches tall, and had died of blunt force trauma to the back of her head. She had dark hair that had been dyed blonde. She'd been in the ground for about six months. What was left of her clothes was a red tracksuit with a white stripe down each side, and she had on a black top underneath. She wore size six trainers. There were cuts and bruises to her arms, legs and upper body, and marks around her wrists and ankles. She had the tattoo of a swallow on her left shoulder.

-X-

A black Range Rover Evoque with private number

plates crawled through the city centre. The driver had picked its passenger up from a large waterside home. A four bedroom, detached house with manicured lawns leading down to the river. The front was electrically gated with high walls. The house was a long way from the terraced, two up-two down council house on the Thelwell Estate that the owner had grown up in.

The driver turned the Range Rover into the car park at the back of the council offices, parking up close to the main doors. They weren't going to stay long.

Getting out he went round to the back of the car and opened up the rear passenger door. Jimmy Russell got out and stood to straighten his suit jacket and tie. He nodded to Ray, the driver, and after locking the car, both strode purposefully into the council building.

Standing in the foyer they were approached by a smart looking lady who'd just left the meeting they were interested in, wearing a lanyard, who in passing pressed a note into Jimmy's hand. He looked at it and nodded. Turning, he threw the note into a nearby bin, storming his way back out to his car.

CHAPTER SEVENTEEN

Monteith was back at the casino talking to the security guards and floorwalkers in the bar.

The sight of Ray struggling to keep up with Jimmy as they flew past him and up to the offices caught Monteith's eye. He decided it was best to carry on with what he was doing as he would find out soon enough what had happened. Both Ray and Lex, slowly at first, were beginning to trust Monteith with some of the ongoings within the Russell Empire. Not the big stuff. They were not stupid.

-X-

In his office, Jimmy grabbed a drink and flung himself onto the large leather sofa.

'I take it it didn't go in our favour?' Allan commented from one of the large armchairs.

'You got that right. It's been pushed to a subcommittee. The police want more information on it. Said, they were not happy at a licence being granted.'

'I thought Spedding said it would pass easily?'

'Well, he was wrong!' Jimmy got up and started to

pace up and down the office. 'That jerk is starting to piss me off.'

'Everybody seems to be pissing you off lately,' Allan said from behind a newspaper.

'What's that meant to mean?' Jimmy turned to face Allan.

Allan moved the paper so he could see Jimmy, 'Just that! You're snapping at people for the smallest of things. You had a go at Lex the other day because he spilled something on your precious carpet.'

'I know, I know. I'm sorry.' Jimmy sat back down on the armchair next to Allan. 'You have always tried to keep me in check when I go off on one. You are my conscience, my dear brother, and I am grateful for that. God knows where I would be without you.'

'So what do you want to do with Spedding?' Allan asked.

Jimmy thought hard. His hands to his face in a triangle, mulling things over. 'I think we need to pay him a little visit. Remind him of his obligations.'

Allan nodded in support. 'Good thinking, brother.'

-X-

Monteith was walking back towards the lift as Ray exited one of them, looking frazzled.

'What's up with the boss?' Monteith asked.

'Tonight's going to be tough,' Ray replied.

Monteith didn't understand.

'When things don't go right for the boss then everyone gets it, even when it's not your fault,' Ray explained.

As they walked between the open double doors leading to the kitchen Lex appeared, munching on an apple. 'Well?'

'He's up there having a go at Allan,' Ray replied.

'Brilliant,' Lex sighed, throwing the apple core in a nearby bin.

'Does this often happen?' Monteith asked.

Lex looked at Ray as if seeking his approval to speak to an 'ex'-copper before responding. 'No, it does not happen too often,' he replied, finally. 'You saw the plans for a gentleman's private club on one of your last visits before you joined us?'

Monteith nodded. 'I vaguely remember them. Why?'

Ray poured himself a coffee. 'Well, there seems to be one obstacle which is proving hard to remove. And when the boss is not happy everyone suffers until things are put right.'

Monteith shook his head while getting himself a drink. 'Thanks for the heads-up. I will stay looking at my screens tonight. If you want somewhere to hide you know where to come.'

'Right I've got work to do,' Lex said to monteith before disappearing.

Monteith turned to Ray. 'What did I do or say to upset him?'

Ray laughed. 'It's not personal. He hates all police, past and present.'

They both walked into the casino. Ray continued as they went. 'Story goes that his dad was a leading detective in the big smoke somewhere. He took his own life after being accused of being involved in a police protection racket. He denied it, but was found guilty. They found him hanging in his cell six months into his sentence. He was still pleading his innocence. Alex doted on his dad and went off the rails after his death. He served five years for GBH on a policeman. After coming out he moved here and started working for the Russells.'

Before Monteith could ask about Ray's

background, the lift doors opened and the Russell brothers stepped out. Allan signalled to Ray.

'Looks like I am required. No rest for the wicked.' Putting down his cup, Ray followed his bosses.

'Wicked is right,' Monteith said to himself.

CHAPTER EIGHTEEN

Watson sat behind his new desk. Being Detective Inspector, if only an acting one, brought with it an office. An office he did not feel comfortable in. Although his office was next to the DCI's and he could see out into the incident room, he still wanted to be out there with his fellow officers. In here he felt out of the way. He preferred being on the front line.

Lorimer stuck his head around the door while putting his jacket on. Watson could see French also rushing to get out.

'Got a sighting of our couple of fraudsters,' Lorimer spat. 'Shopping centre at the Meadows. Security is keeping tabs on them until we arrive.'

Taking his coffee cup, Watson went across to the information boards holding the latest information of the main investigations they were working on. Mac's report and photos from the autopsy of the buried body had been sent through. As he put the new information up DCI Wright stood beside him.

'There are still no sightings of Alison Grant. PC Walsh was given his orders to leave last night by Mr Grant. Something about upsetting his wife, which I don't believe from what Sharon told me. He is just a control freak.'

'No missing persons matching the description of the body found yet either,' he added.

-X-

Lorimer and French arrived at the Meadows Shopping Centre, parking as instructed round the back in the employees' car park. The Head of Security was waiting by the entrance to escort them into the CCTV room. A bank of thirty screens filled one wall, giving the operators a view to both entrances of the shopping centre, the main concourse, and the front of each shop. There were also a few covering the insides of the high street supermarket which covered the largest unit.

'Where are they?' Lorimer asked.

'There,' The CCTV operator zoomed in to offer them a close-up of the pair sitting on a bench.

'Have they bought anything?' French asked.

'Only drinks, and they paid cash for them. We checked,' the security guard said.

'Looks like we have movement', the operator said, pointing at the screen. The couple were now walking into the supermarket.

'How do you want to play this?' the security guard asked.

'We cannot arrest them until they have paid for the goods using, hopefully, the stolen debit card. Keep your distance till then. DC French and I are going to do a bit of shopping.'

CHAPTER NINETEEN

Don Spedding exited the council offices and walked across to his car. Approaching, he saw a black Range Rover Evoke parked next to his. Leaning against the front of it was Ray. Don knew why he was there, but it did not stop him from thinking of making a run for it. Turning he came face to face with Allan Russell.

Allan put a hand around Don's shoulders as if they had been friends for years. 'My brother would like a quick chat with you,' he said, frogmarching him towards the Range Rover. Ray opened the back door.

'Get in,' Jimmy Russell snapped.

Don slowly stepped up and slid across the leather seat next to Jimmy, Allan following so Don had nowhere to move. Ray closed the door, staying outside.

Jimmy kept his gaze forward. 'What happened?'

Don visibly shivered. His throat became suddenly dry. 'Sorry, Mr Russell. I could not stop it from being referred to the subcommittee. The majority went with the police's concerns over licencing and wanted to look into the proposal closer. I fought for you to get it through but . . .'

Russell put his hand up. 'I have had enough of

your whining.' Looking straight at Don, 'You make sure it gets through next time. Am I clear!'

'I will try my best, but it won't be easy,' Don squeaked out.

Allan reached forward into the pocket behind the driver's seat and pulled out a large envelope, handing it to Don. 'I don't think your wife would be happy seeing these.'

Don opened it to find four ten by eight inch colour photos of Don with a female in uncompromising positions over his office desk.

-X-

Watson sat in his car outside St Mary's sixth form school close to the end of the school day. Noticing that the road had started to grow busier, Watson got out and stood by his car. Parents in oversized cars, trying to get as close to the gates as they could for their precious kids not to have to walk so far, were causing traffic to build up.

The bell rang and a swarm of children came flying out of the school. It was not long before he spotted who it was he had come to see. Marcus crossed the road just down from where he was standing, with a group of his friends. Watson called out after him and moved towards the group, gracing them with a flash of his ID card.

'Detective, have you found her?' Marcus was quick to ask.

'No, sorry, not yet. You haven't heard from her either, I take it?'

'No. We're going to look for her this evening,' Marcus added, his five friends nodding along.

'You should talk to that trainer at the athletics club, Ian Fellows, creepy,' one of the young women called out.

'Oh, I forgot about that. Yeah, Alison's coach was being a bit overly friendly with her and a few of the others. Alison told me that there was nothing to it and that we should stop worrying, but his behaviour made me uncomfortable.'

'What was he doing?'

'He would take them out for extra training; the county trials are coming up,' he shrugged.

CHAPTER TWENTY

Watson, driving back to HQ saw Joseph Clayton standing near the bus stop. Clayton was looking all of his seventy-plus years: tired and haggard. Life has not been good to him over recent times. And chasing after his two loony sons did not help.

Watson turned his car around and pulled up next to Joseph. He wound down the side window. 'Need a lift anywhere?'

'Oh, Mr Watson. Yes, thanks for the offer, I'm off back home.' Joseph picked up his shopping and walking cane and got in the front passenger seat. 'You're a saviour, Mr Watson. The buses can be a pain, especially when they are busy. The young people don't have respect for the elderly. Not bothering to get up when there are no seats so we can sit down.'

Watson signalled to move back into the traffic. 'Where're your boys, Davy and Billy? Don't they help you out, give you a lift into town?'

Joseph grunted. 'They're off doing their own things. Anyway, on my own I can go and have a quick pint and a bet on the horses.'

Watson laughed.

'How's your family?' Joseph enquired.

'Very well thank you. Jason turned twelve the other day.'

'Really! How time flies.' Joseph shook his head.

Watson drove on for a couple of minutes before entering the Thelwell Estate where Joseph lived. As they did Joseph turned to him. 'I hear you're having another go at the Russells again?'

'Don't know what you have heard but . . .'

'Oh, come now, Mr Watson. The grapevine is long and healthy at the moment. There is nothing which gets past it nowadays.'

'Sorry, Joseph, cannot comment on what you have heard.'

'Is that why Mr Monteith has not been around for a while?'

Watson glanced at him. 'No comment.'

'Suit yourself,' Joseph said with a big grin. Watson pulled into Mr Clayton's street and parked outside his house. 'Can you help me in with my shopping, I feel a little out of breath?'

Watson smiled. 'Go and open the door, I'll grab your bags.' The curtains were twitching in the neighbouring houses as Watson made his way into the property. Joseph was standing at the window.

'I would just love to give them something to really get the gossipers going. Standing fully naked in front of my bedroom window would do it.'

'And you would end up with time in our cells and a trip to court. Now, where do you want this shopping?'

'It's my house I can walk around naked if I want. On the kitchen side, and put the kettle on while you are at it.'

Watson walked back into the front room. 'The kettle's on and I need to get going.'

Joseph was sat in his chair by the fireplace. 'Hang

on a minute, Mr Watson.' Watson turned to Joseph as he continued. 'Can you go into my bureau behind my chair, second draw down there is an envelope marked confidential.'

Watson did as instructed and passed it to Joseph. 'No, you take it, Mr Watson, it's for you and your team.'

'What's in it?' Watson asked, as he sat down.

Joseph took a big breath and looked straight at Watson. 'If you are looking to take down the Russells, what's in there will hopefully help you. I've known the Russells since they arrived here in the 1970s. Their father was not a man to cross. And his sons, as you know, carried on the tradition. In that envelope are photocopies of a book I have stashed away. My insurance, so to speak. What you have there are details of the Russells' activities I have collected over the years. Loose lips in the pub bragging, petty feuds. Some you may know about but could not pin on them. Some . . . Well, have a read.'

CHAPTER TWENTY-ONE

Watson exited the lift and walked into the CDA office, hoping for a quick getaway after updating the boards on what Marcus and his friends had told him about Ian Fellows.

The others were gathered around in a group with Lorimer and French holding court.

'Did I miss much?' Watson asked.

The group parted to show the state Lorimer was in. His hair, face, jacket, and white top was now a lovely colour purple.

'What the hell happened to you?' Watson exclaimed.

'Beetroot!,' Lorimer replied.

'Pardon?'

'Beetroot, I am covered in beetroot juice.'

'I hate to ask why?' Watson sat on the edge of a desk waiting to be given the story.

'Those credit card fraudsters did not want to come in peacefully. Well one of them didn't. We had him down one of the isles when he picked up a large jar of beetroot and chucked it at us. It smashed against part of the racking, covering me and one of the security guards.'

French, trying to keep a straight face, continued the tale, 'We managed to catch him when he rounded the end of another isle straight into an abandoned trolley. They are both in the cells downstairs. We will interview them later when the duty solicitor arrives.'

Watson burst out laughing. 'You had better hope none of that was filmed and ends up of Facebook or YouTube.'

French turned to Lorimer, 'Come on beetroot juice, you had better get yourself cleaned up before the interview.'

As the two of them left the office, Watson made his way over to the information board and put Ian Fellows' name and a question mark against Alison Grant's disappearance.

'Someone, we know?' DCI Wright joined him.

'Spoke to the boyfriend, Marcus, and some of Alison's friends. Fellows came up in conversation. He's Alison's coach at the athletics club. They said he was giving a little more attention to Alison and some of the other young women at the club.' Looking at the board containing a photograph of the body from the industrial estate he asked, 'Any of the local tattooists recognise their handiwork?'

'No luck there as of yet,' Wright replied. 'Swallows are common apparently.'

'Yeah but every tattooist has their own style.'

'We'll get a hook – eventually.'

'Just got to keep throwing out the bait.'

'Oh, and Mac rang with an update. He has sent X-rays and impressions to local dentists.'

'Hopefully we will get a hit,' Watson replied.

DC Sandall was returning to his desk with a fresh cup of coffee. 'Paul, can you look for details on this Ian Fellows. Local Athletics coach. Someone Alison's friends have mentioned.'

'On it.'

Twenty minutes later, Sandall knocked on Watson's door. 'Have you a minute?'

'Yes, sure. Is it about Ian Fellows?'

Sandall sat down. 'When I was checking HOLMES his name was flagged up.'

'In connection to what?' Watson asked.

'The county force is interested in him.' Sandall passed over the details. 'Looks like they have an ongoing investigation. That's who to contact.'

'Jeff Johnson, I know him. Thanks Paul, I'll give him a ring.'

CHAPTER TWENTY-TWO

TUESDAY 10.30 p.m.

Monteith was tucked away in his office skimming the screens in front of him. The casino was quiet, it being the beginning of the week. Most of the money was made Thursday, Friday and the weekend. This was when the high rollers came to play. The restaurant and bar helped cover the cost of keeping the doors open for the rest of the week. Waitresses mingled with customers playing the fruit machines, serving drinks and bar snacks to the gullible and desperate, hoping to win the big jackpot. Over on the big tables drinks could be served but food was not allowed. The restaurant had a good reputation because the Russells employed top chefs and only a select few could book a table. Only the highest of society could afford to bring their clients here to be wined and dined.

How many of them did the Russells have in their pocket? Monteith mused as he tucked into his chicken and chips, which he washed down with a bottle of still water.

He heard the security pad for the door of the office being used before Allan Russell entered.

'Everything okay?' Allan asked, as he walked

towards Monteith.

'Yep,' Monteith replied between mouthfuls.

'Has your brother calmed down?'

'Yes, he has,' Allan replied.

Monteith's eye was drawn towards the screen. Among the jackpot machines a smartly dressed man who had been playing for over an hour grabbed one of the waitresses and yelled at her for another drink. She hollered for support, and before you could shout 'full house' two of the security guards covering the floor appeared. They asked him to leave but he replied with a torrent of drunken abuse so they grabbed him and threw him out.

Then down by the toilets, a young lad in a denim jacket and red baseball cap appeared to be checking the place out as if planning to do something in the ruckus.

Allan spotted him too and was on the radio in seconds, requesting the security guards get down there.

Monteith and Allan saw the lad pass a small pack of something to another lad going into the toilet. Quickly followed by another package to a lady exiting the women's.

'The cheeky bastard,' Allan exclaimed.

Allan flew out of the room.

Monteith watched what was unfolding on the screens. Three security guards converged on the unsuspecting, stupid Monteith thought, lad just as he was doing another deal. Seeing the guards the lad tried to make his escape, rounding a corner he ran straight into the unwelcoming grip of Lex.

'Well, Well, Well. Who do we have here?' Lex had the lad in an arm lock as the guards arrived.

'Get the fuck off me.' The lad wrestled to get free.

'Who are you?' Lex asked.

Allan Russell walked up beside Lex. He looked at the lad who was squirming to free himself. 'You were asked a question. It would be best if you answered him.'

'Wayne – argh – Marsh.'

'Let go of him,' he instructed Lex.

Lex released Wayne, who began to rub his shoulder furiously.

'I saw what you were up to on our CCTV cameras.' Allan pointed up to a nearby one. 'Now show me what you have in your pockets.'

'I don't have anything,' Wayne squirmed.

'Don't insult me.'

Lex stepped forward.

Wayne huffed and reached inside his jacket, retrieving five small bags of pills – ecstasy probably – and a wad of cash.

Allan signalled for him to hand them over, which he did reluctantly.

'Hey, that's my money give it back,' Wayne shouted.

Allan put a finger to his mouth as if to say shut it.

'One thing I hate is drugs. Another is people like you thinking it's alright to sell drugs in my establishment. I'm taking the cash as recompense. You're lucky I am only doing this. Lex, will you show out.'

Two of the guards moved behind Wayne and began to lead him towards the rear exit.

Allan stopped Lex at the door. 'You know what to do.'

Lex nodded and followed them out.

Monteith had been watching all of this on the screens. He had also seen the three people who the lad had given the drugs to getting picked up and thrown out of the front door.

He switched between cameras catching the man being forced to swallow the pills in the floodlit backyard.

The office door opened. Monteith turned his attention to the monitor focused on the casino proper, but not quickly enough.

Allan strode purposefully into the room.

'I will keep an eye out in case he turns up again,' Monteith said.

'No need. He won't be coming back.' Allan smiled, before turning to exit the office.

CHAPTER TWENTY-THREE

TUESDAY 11.20 p.m.

Watson sat looking at the envelope that Joseph Clayton had entrusted him with. He turned it over in his hands.

'It's not going to open itself.'

Watson glanced up to see Sally leaning against the doorframe.

'What is it anyway?'

Watson put the envelope down. 'Something Joseph Clayton gave me earlier. Said it had something to do with the Russells.'

'Everything at the moment seems to have something to do with that family,' Sally said, matter-of-factly. 'Keith and Katie would still be together if it wasn't for them. She's in bits over at her mum's. And the kids cannot understand why daddy is not with them.'

Watson got up from his desk. And put his arms around Sally. 'It's complicated.'

'Try telling that to Katie and the kids.'

'Keith did. It was Katie's choice to move out.'

'So it was Katie's fault was it?'

'No, I didn't say that. Keith was put in a no-win situation.'

'Well, he wouldn't have been put in that situation if it wasn't for his gambling.'

'You'll not get an argument from me over that.' Watson pulled Sally close and gave her a hug. 'Listen, why we are getting het up over this. I can think of something better to do.' He kissed her passionately on the lips.

'Oh you can, can you?'

Watson moved to Sally's neck and gave it a peck.

Sally moaned softly. 'You better follow me then.' Taking his hand and walking towards the stairs.

CHAPTER TWENTY-FOUR

WEDNESDAY 8.30 A.M

DCI Wright sat behind her desk looking out at the main office. Less than two months ago she was brought in by Superintendent Matthews to take over the Criminal Detective Agency. A career officer, she had forgone raising a family to concentrate on getting as high as she could in the force. Now in her mid-forties, she had achieved just that.

Before her, she could see a group of talented officers who would back each other to the ends of the earth. Acting DI Terry Watson and DS Keith Monteith were as close to each other without being married. Newly promoted DS Karl Lorimer was becoming another strong member of the team and was beginning to forge a good partnership with DC Emma French. Last but not least was DC Paul Sandall. Slowly getting his feet under the table, he'd come up front in collecting data and disseminating information to those who needed it while they were searching for Monteith.

As long as she could keep Matthews from sticking his nose in too much, she was certain that this team could grow from strength to strength.

Picking up her notes and her mug of coffee, she

strolled into the main office and stood next to the board containing the outstanding crimes which were being worked on.

'Right ladies and gentlemen let's get this briefing going. Karl and Emma, where are we?'

Emma stood up. 'The pair were interviewed and charged last night with five counts of debit card fraud. They are due in court this afternoon.'

'Excellent!'

She turned to Watson. 'What's the update on Alison Grant?'

'Still no positive word from uniform.'

A phone went off from somewhere in the room. DC Sandall picked it up.

Wright continued, 'The body?'

'No word from the dentist yet, boss.'

'Boss?' DC Sandall said. 'That was downstairs. Railway maintenance this morning found a body of a girl in the bushes on one of the embankments. She was wearing a tracksuit.'

CHAPTER TWENTY-FOUR

WEDNESDAY 9 .a.m.

Sharon Walsh parked her Mini Countryman outside the Grants' house. She had been waiting for David to leave for work before approaching the property. During her last visit, when Alison was reported missing, she was unceremoniously told to leave by Mr Grant and didn't want to bump into him again.

She walked up the driveway and pressed the doorbell. Joan opened it, face tear-stained, still wearing a dressing gown.

'Mrs Grant, are you okay?' Sharon asked. Joan nodded slowly, opened the door and made her way back into the front room. Sharon closed the door behind her and entered the living room. 'Mrs Grant?'

'Have you found her?' Joan was sat on the sofa.

'No, I'm sorry, I haven't heard anything.' Sharon sat on the edge of a chair facing Joan.

'I just thought that's why you came round,' Joan said in a disappointed tone.

'I came to see how you, your husband and Alex were doing, and also to see if you had heard from her.'

Joan shook her head. 'No. Marcus came over last night, said he and a few of their friends were going out looking again, but they didn't find her.'

'Listen, Joan, why don't you go and get yourself changed, and I will put the kettle on?' Sharon smiled, trying to put her at ease.

Joan nodded and made her way towards the stairs.

Sharon got two mugs ready then, walking back into the living room hearing the shower running, she took the opportunity to look around the front room. Photos of family holidays, that looked like they'd been taken a number of years ago. The obligatory school year photos with both Alison and Alex sitting proud and grinning like Cheshire cats. Unusual ornaments.

Hearing the shower being switched off and realising the kettle must have boiled, she turned to the kitchen and started to pour the drinks.

'That's better,' Joan said, as she entered the kitchen.

'Just looking at your garden - very nice,' Sharon commented, handing a mug of tea to Joan.

'Thank you. I am the green-fingered one. David is always busy with work. If he's not at the office he is away at some meeting or other.' Joan sat down at the kitchen table cupping the mug in her hands, not looking up.

'Is he away often?' Sharon was leaning, back against the sink.

'At least two weeks a month. He's been working hard trying to keep the business going.'

'That's Argent Logistics?'

Joan nodded. 'It's been tough over the last year. I don't know much about it, but the snippets of phone calls David gets even during the evening from people suggests things are not going so well. Possible takeover I heard him say once.'

'When we were here last time, your husband

seemed . . .' Sharon paused, thinking of the correct wording, 'Hostile, angry even?'

'He was being an arsehole,' Joan said. 'I rang him at work, which he was pissed off about. When he got home we had a blazing row. He was just about to go into a big important meeting with a client and I had probably ruined any chance of a deal.' Joan tensed up as she spoke.

'Wasn't he at all worried about Alison going missing?'

'No, not David. He dismissed my concern, said she would come home when she was ready. He only has time for his precious job. Has been like that for the last year.'

Sharon could see the dam Joan built to contain her feelings was about to burst. 'Before the last twelve months was he–'

'A normal, husband and father?' Joan finished her sentence for her. 'Yes. He was very supportive of Alison and Alex in whatever they were doing. We used to go to watch Alison running and Alex playing rugby for their schools at the weekend. But now, he hardly has time for us. It's all work, work, work. I did try and talk to him about it, but now I have given up.'

Sharon moved and sat down at the table opposite Joan. Before her sat a wife, mother and homemaker, living as though she is the only parent, bringing up two kids.

'How was Alison before she disappeared? Was she worried about anything?'

Joan thought. 'No, she was her normal self. Concentrating on training, running the half-marathon to raise money for breast cancer. Her Aunt, my sister, died six months ago from it. I think she had close to a thousand pounds in sponsorship.

'I'm sorry about your sister.'

'The end was a bit of a blessing, she was in a lot of pain.'

As they re-entered the living room Sharon's phone started to ring. Taking it out of her bag she moved to the front window to answer it.

Joan sat down on the sofa looking towards Sharon as she spoke. The look on her face as she turned to Joan told her all she needed to know.

CHAPTER TWENTY-FIVE

'Police tape decorated the area, flapping away in the wind. It ran for fifty metres alongside the road which ran beside the railway embankment. The road had been blocked off at either end, the traffic diverted through a nearby village. The railway line had also been closed for the time-being, which was causing even more disruption to the already pissed off commuters.

Police vehicles, CSI vans, and Mac's morgue bus filled the street. On the grassy verge of the track, the British rail maintenance workers were giving their statements to a couple of police officers. Crime Scene Investigators were searching along the curb-side embankment in search of anything significant.

DI Watson parked his Ford Focus behind one of the police cars. He was with PC Paul Sandall, Watson and DCI Wright agreeing it would be good for him to get out of the office. Both stood looking down towards where the body of the woman had been found, among thick hawthorn bushes and long grass.

Mac and the CSI team had somehow managed to erect a tent over the body within the bushes. Watson and Sandall signed in with a PC to register their presence, before making their way through the police cordon where they came to stand as close as they were allowed.

'Watson! We meet again.' Mac said, looking up, catching the knowing expression on his face, he added, 'You know who we have here?'

'Alison Grant,' Watson replied with a sigh. 'She went missing on Monday while out for a run. Uniform gave us a description of the clothing she's wearing. I've been sent to confirm.'

'Here,' he called over the man snapping photos of the body. The man whizzed through a few shots to show him a close-up of the woman.

Alison was lying on her side with her arms in front of her, still wearing her tracksuit and trainers.

'That's her alright,' he nodded. 'How did she die?'

'Hit on the back of the head here.' Mac pointed to his crown. 'Been tied up at some point, there are abrasions on her wrists and ankles. I will get a better view back at the morgue.'

'Was she killed here or elsewhere and brought here?'

'Elsewhere then dumped. The wound at the back of her head is a couple of days old by the look of it. And there is no blood spatter on anything surrounding her.'

'Do you have a time of death?' Watson asked.

'Possibly twelve to eighteen hours? Rigor had set in, but it's releasing its grip. I will have a better timescale later.'

'Thanks, Mac.'

Surveying the area, Watson spotted a uniformed officer leaving the maintenance workers who had begun to pack up and move off. Watson recognised him as PC Gary Kendall, from his initial visit to the Grant residence.

'Good to see you again.'

'How did the maintenance workers find her?'

'They were clearing up the line and surrounding area of rubbish which can be a hazard to trains. One of the men nipped up behind a hedge to take a leak. He found her on his way back down. Almost fell over her due to the dark. They rang the yard who contacted us.'

'So she was likely left here sometime yesterday evening or early this morning?'

'Looks like it.' Kendall agreed.

CHAPTER TWENTY-SIX

Sharon had brought Joan in to the viewing gallery. Watson and Sandall stood beside them, noting their reaction. No-one had yet been able to get hold of David. Lorimer and French had been sent over to his workplace to see if he was there.

Joan stood in front of the curtains as they were drawn back covering the glass. She screamed and began sobbing uncontrollably, before collapsing to the ground. Sharon knelt down and hugged her.

Watson walked into Mac's office a minute later. 'It never gets any easier.' He slumped onto a battered chair in the corner.

'Where is the mother?' Mac poured them each a mug of coffee.

'Sharon and Paul have taken her to the comfort room.'

Mac handed a mug to Watson, 'Is the father around?'

'Work. Keith and Emma have gone to see if they can find him.'

'You should keep an eye on Paul. Very interested in pathology.'

'We will send him to all the autopsies from now

on.'

'Just because you and Monteith got squeamish with that bloater the other month.'

'That was Monteith, I was alright.'

'Yer right, which was why you were over the other side of the room for most of it.'

'At least I stayed in the room, Keith was so green the boss had to send him home when we got back.' Both broke into laughter which was immediately broken by Paul, who stuck his head around the door.

'Sharon's taking Mrs Grant home.'

'Good. Mac is it alright for Paul to stay for Alison's autopsy?' Watson winked at Mac.

'Me?' Paul exclaimed.

'Yes, is that okay?'

'I would love to.'

'See, he would an all.'

'Can't I?'

'No. Unfortunately only senior officers such as myself are allowed to observe.'

Mac, grinning, searched his desk and pulled out a file from a pile. 'Got sent an x-ray by email.' He handed the file to Watson. 'The body. Her name is Claire Townsend. Her dentist is local, and last saw her three months ago.'

'Thanks, Mac. We can compare her stats to missing persons now we know she lived in the city.'

As they left the office, another gurney was being brought in by Mac's assistant. He handed Mac the paperwork. 'Who have we here? Ah, the teenager found in the park this morning. Suspected drug overdose. On his person was identification for a Wayne Marsh. Well, Wayne, welcome to my humble abode.'

Paul nudged Watson, 'Does he always talk to them?'

'Yep, and sings to them sometimes.'

CHAPTER TWENTY-SEVEN

Watson arrived back at the agency HQ by mid-afternoon. By 3 p.m. the whiteboards had been updated with the new information gathered on both the Alison Grant and Claire Townsend murders.

DCI Wright stood in front of the boards waiting for the remaining seats to be taken by uniformed officers who had been seconded to the agency for the duration of the search. The room was filled with the sound of scraping chairs, and chatter.

Watson was at his desk gathering his thoughts while staring at the envelope Joseph Clayton had given him.

'Ladies and gentlemen, could I have your attention please,' DCI Wright said. She The pointed to a photograph of Alison which had been given to them by her mother. 'Alison went missing on Monday morning while on a training run. She was found this morning on a railway embankment to the north of the city. We need to find those people living on the route she is supposed to have taken we haven't yet been able to speak to.' She pointed at a map of the city's northern district. Alison's typical routes marked out.

Turning around Wright asked Lorimer, 'Karl what's the update on David Grant, Alison's father? Have we heard from him yet?'

DS Karl Lorimer stood. 'Emma and I went to Argent Logistics where Mr Grant works. His PA said he had gone to see a client out of the city. She tried to get hold of him while we were there, but his phone kept going to voicemail. She said she would contact us if she managed to get through to him.'

'Thanks, Karl. Is Sharon still at the Grants' house?'

'I believe so boss.'

'Good, so if he turns up there we are covered. Right, next to the boyfriend, Marcus Devonport. Terry, you spoke to him last, what do you make of him?'

Watson sat on the edge of his desk. 'He seemed genuinely upset at Alison's disappearance. He's been nothing short of helpful and engaging and has been actively searching for her.'

'Where have we got with this Ian Fellows fella?'

'Spoke to DI Jeff Johnson at county. They have an ongoing operation, ORACLE, Fellows is on their radar. According to Jeff, Fellows wasn't in West Ravenswood when Alison went missing. He was at work in the south of the county. Paul has updated HOLMES with what Marcus and Alison's friends have said about Fellows.'

'So, he's not our murderer?'

'Sounds like he's a lot of things, *but* a murderer.'

DCI Wright took a quick mouthful of coffee before continuing. 'Claire Townsend.' A photograph of the woman from missing persons had been put up on the board following her identification. 'Emma, you have the details?'

DC Emma French stood. 'Claire Townsend, age twenty-four, went missing three months ago. Her body was found buried at Copeland industrial estate under the floor of one of the units. She was wrapped in carpet. I will be disclosing the news to her husband later today with a liaison officer.'

'Do we know who owned the unit prior to the developers moving in?'

'A national tyre, brakes and exhaust company. I'm awaiting a call from their HQ with the date of when they shut up shop and a list of employees that worked there.'

'Thank you, Emma. Well, that's all folks.'

Right after she'd distributed jobs for everyone to be getting on with Watson moved towards her. 'Can I have a word?' He nodded towards her office.

Watson shut the door behind him. Wright topped up her coffee and sat behind her desk. 'What's up Terry?' she asked.

He sat down opposite her with the envelope in his hands. 'I bumped into Joseph Clayton yesterday. He was waiting by the bus stop with his shopping so I gave him a lift home. While I was there, he was asking me about the Russells. I did not tell him anything, obviously. But he gave me this. It's a copy. Said the original is stashed away somewhere for insurance. Said it contains things about the Russells' activities from first hand or overheard. I have not looked at it. Thought, I should hand it over to you, boss.'

'Do you think what he had put in that envelope is true or made up?' Wright said sceptically.

'I have known Joseph for as long as I have been here and, although his family aren't always on the right side of the law, Joseph is as straight as they come.' He handed the envelope over.

'And you only thought about giving me this now?'

'I'm sorry, but with everything that's going on with the other cases, it slipped my mind.'

'I could have you suspended for this, Terry. Withholding information,' Wright said forcefully.

'I know, I know. I screwed up.'

'Have you looked at it?'

Watson shook his head. 'I wanted to show you and Matthews first.'

Wright slowly nodded. 'Leave this with me. Matthews is not in the office now. I'll take a look at it and if anything in it needs acting on, I'll pass it up to him. What are you doing now?'

'We are picking up Alison's boyfriend and one of her other friends. We need to go over a few things with them.'

'Have they been told about the discovery of Alison's body?'

'PC Walsh said that Joan phoned Marcus when they returned home after identifying Alison.'

'Okay.'

Wright took a moment to think. 'You look after it. Joseph gave it to you. Lock it in a drawer somewhere and we will deal with it when we have more time. Let's sort out what we have on our plates first.'

Watson agreed and walked into his office, opened the bottom drawer of his desk placing the envelope at the back under a number of files. Locking it, he picked up his jacket and went to meet PC Kendall. They had a Marcus Devonport to interview.

CHAPTER TWENTY-EIGHT

Monteith stood by his car looking at the house he was parked in front of, owned by his mother-in-law, where his wife and children were currently staying. Katie had moved out of their home soon after he'd mentioned he was leaving the force and had told her that he was now going to be working for the Russells. Gambling away their savings and becoming indebted to them was one thing. But going to work for them was quite another. They hadn't spoken to each other, and he hadn't seen his kids since they'd left.

Walking up to the front door his boots weighed as much as lead. Knocking on the door and waiting for an answer was agonising. He heard laughter from behind the door, kids' laughter.

The door opened and Katie stood there. 'What do you want?' she spat.

'To talk, to see the kids.'

'We don't have anything to talk about. You have chosen your friends over us,' Katie said matter-of-factly.

'Believe me, there wasn't much of a choice.'

'Daddy!' Pixie screamed with delight, moving towards the door.

Monteith picked Pixie up and hugged her close.

'When are we coming home?' Pixie asked.

Monteith looked at his wife before answering. 'Mummy and daddy have to talk about working that out. That's why I'm here, as well as to see you and Rachael.'

Katie's thunderous face was replaced by a false smile.

'Can I come in?' Monteith asked, knowing that she could not do anything else but let him now he was holding Pixie.

Katie stood back as he carried Pixie into the living room.

Once drinks were made and Rachael and Pixie had spent ten minutes with their daddy, Katie's mother took the girls into the garden, leaving Katie and Monteith to sort out their differences. They were sat opposite each other at the dining room table, from where they could see the kids playing in the back garden.

'I love you and the kids, and being away from you all is tearing me apart.' Monteith started.

'Quit working for the Russells and find another security job. There is plenty out there,' replied Katie.

'I can't do that,' Monteith said, shaking his head.

'Well, then we have nothing more to say to each other.' Katie stood up.

'Sit down!' Monteith growled.

'What?' Katie asked, wide-eyed, mouth hung in askance.

'I said sit down,' he spoke in a lighter tone. 'I need you to know why I cannot do what you have asked me to.'

Katie slowly sat back down. 'Terry, you're frightening me.'

'Just hear me out, and if you still feel the way you

do then . . .' Monteith's voice faded away. Katie nodded her head in a reluctant manner.

Monteith took a swig of his coffee. 'None of this goes outside these four walls, okay?'

She nodded.

'I cannot quit working for the Russells because I'm working for them as undercover police officer. They have no idea I'm still on the forces payroll.'

Katie looked like she had been slapped across the face.

'Before the Russells abducted me, Superintendent Matthews wanted me to get closer to the Russells to gather information so we could bring down their operation. Inside information.'

Katie went to speak, but Monteith put his hand up to stop her. 'Let me continue, then if you have any questions I will try and answer them. Matthews threatened to put me back on the beat if I refused. Then they abducted me and offered me a position I wasn't able to refuse, less they make my life and that of my family's difficult, to head the security at their casino. It was an indirect threat against you, Katie, and the kids.'

Katie gasped and broke down in tears. Monteith got up and went round to try and comfort her, but she shrugged him off.

He reluctantly sat back down and continued. 'Then I woke up in hospital.'

Katie wiped her eyes and sat back, staring at her husband.

'When I told DCI Wright, she, Terry, and the others were about to arrest them for my abduction, but Matthews wanted me to take them up on their offer. It was this or I'd be out of a job, and you know how much my career means to me.'

'How long are you going to be working for the

Russells?'

'Until we have enough on them to charge them with something that'll release their stranglehold on this city.'

Katie got up and stood at the window. Rachael and Pixie were playing chase with her mother. Laughter permeated through the glass.

Monteith joined her.

CHAPTER TWENTY-NINE

'Get me whoever is in charge of this place,' David Grant boomed at the top of his voice to anyone who could hear him, standing in the middle of the reception area at the police headquarters. 'I want them down here, now!' he continued, pointing his finger first at the desk and then to his feet.

'Sir, if you calm down–'

'Calm down? My daughter has been murdered and I only found out about it when I came home. I need to see someone to make a complaint about the incompetence in this place.' By the time David Grant had finished he was leaning towards the desk sergeant eyeball to eyeball.

The officer took a step back asked for his name.

Given it, he said, 'I will make enquires upstairs to see who it is you need to see. Please give me a moment.'

'I want to see the head of this tin pot shambles.'

The officer retreated several feet to make the call. He'd already been warned Mr Grant might make an entrance.

Ten minutes later, DCI Wright, along with DC Sandall appeared from the stairwell. Grant was pacing around giving anyone who was looking at him an evil stare.

'Mr Grant?' DCI Wright approached with her hand out straight. Grant took one look at her.

'You in charge?' Grant snapped back.

'DCI Wright and this is DC Sandall. Please follow me. My section is dealing with what you came in about.'

Grant still seething grunted something and strode past her into the office, passing Sandall who held the door open.

Grant stood against the back wall. Wright and Sandall pulled out chairs and sat down at a floor-bolted t able.

'Mr Grant, would you like to take a seat and we will answer any questions you have?' Wright said.

Grant stared at them as if they both had two heads.

'I came home to an inconsolable wife and one of your so-called "family liaison officers" to be told my daughter is dead. And nobody thought fit to contact me?' Grant had taken up an aggressive posture, leaning his hands on the desk.

'Mr Grant, please sit down.'

Grant stood up and whipped a chair away from the desk and sat on it. 'Satisfied?'

'Thank you. Now Mr Grant, first I would like to offer my and my colleagues' condolences on losing your daughter, Alison.'

Grant grunted a reply.

'When we identified Alison's body and your wife told us you were at work, I did send a couple of detectives to your office to let you know. The receptionist said you were out at a meeting and tried on numerous occasions to get you on your mobile phone, but it constantly went to your voicemail. You were uncontactable.'

'Erm yes, I was in a meeting with a client.'

'And this client had no phones at their offices that your receptionist could ring?'

'Erm no, they have just set up. Anyway, what happened to Alison? Where was she? Have you caught the bastard who killed her?'

'She was found on a railway embankment not far from where you live. British rail maintenance workers discovered her this morning. And Mr Grant, I don't believe I said she was murdered.'

Grant's face went bright red with anger.

'DCI Wright, Why are you not out there finding out what happened to her?'

Wright bit her tongue. 'It's early in our enquiries and we have not had the autopsy report back. Until we have that we don't know how she died. Once we have that I can answer some more of your questions.'

'Make sure you do!'

Grant stood, knocked his chair over and stormed out of the office and exited the station.

Sandall looked at Wright. 'But we have the autopsy results. I brought them back with me?'

'Do you think it would be a good idea to tell him in the mood he is in?'

'No, probably not.'

Wright and Sandall got up and made their way out of the office. 'And there's not a chance in hell he was at a work meeting. He wasn't there.'

CHAPTER THIRTY

Watson sat across from Marcus Devonport and Steph Parkinson in one of the vulnerable witness rooms in the station. They had been brought in for an informal chat regarding Alison's death. Watson thought they might open up more in a relaxed environment, instead of an interview room.

Also in the room were their fathers, seated close by. Watson was accompanied by a female PC who was standing by the door.

'Marcus, Steph,' Watson said, 'I have asked you to attend the station because Marcus you were Alison's boyfriend, and Steph you were one of her best friends. You are not under caution and are free to leave at any time. Mr Devonport, Mr Parkinson are you okay with what I have just said?'

All four of them nodded and said yes.

'Okay. Let's go over what we have. Alison left her house at 8.30 a.m. on Monday for a run. She was reported missing two hours later. Early this morning she was found dead on a railway embankment. What we would, and you would I presume, like to find out is what happened to her between those two periods. So any information you have, however irrelevant you think it may be would be greatly appreciated.'

Both glanced at each other so quickly that had he blinked Watson might have missed it, but he didn't. They knew something.

'Marcus, where were you on Monday morning, prior to turning up at Alison's house?'

'I was at home. I had arranged to meet Alison at eleven o'clock before going into town.'

'And when you arrived, what happened?'

'Alison's mum was at the door saying that Alison had not got back and she was worried. I got into my car and went out to look for her.'

'What car do you drive?' Watson asked.

'Erm a Toyota Aygo, why?' Marcus seemed baffled by the question.

'Colour?'

'Silver. It was parked outside the house when you first came that morning.'

'It's so we can discount it if someone remembers seeing a silver Toyota Aygo in the area at that time. We know it could be you that they saw searching.' Watson smiled back at him.

'And Steph where were you on Monday?' Watson switched the questioning to see if he could catch her off-guard.

'Erm, what? Oh, I was at college double maths first thing. Marcus rang me during break to see if Alison had been in touch as she had gone missing.'

'And had she?'

'No. I hadn't talked to her since the evening before, when we were all in town.'

'And how was she?'

Marcus answered the question. 'She was fine, her normal self. Enjoying the night.'

'Until those boys tried to chat her up,' Steph added.

Watson was going to ask about that when there was a commotion outside. Loud voices could be heard. He nodded to the PC who left the room to see what was happening.

'Tried to chat her up?' Watson asked.

'Yes.' Steph continued. 'Typical drunks thinking that every female who's out in a nightclub are free game.

Before Watson could say anything the PC opened the door and signalled to him. He excused himself. In the corridor, he could see a man in reception bellowing. He knew who it was and the reason he was there. Then he spotted Wright and Sandall go over to Grant and take him into a side office. Watson and the PC re-entered the interview room.

'Sorry about that,' Watson said, as he sat back down. 'Alison's father was kicking off.'

Both Marcus and Steph looked at each other with shock on their faces.

'Does he know we're here?' Marcus asked.

'Why do you ask?' Watson queried.

'Because he is a nutter! If he sees us here he will think we had something to do with Alison's death.' Both Marcus and Steph looked scared and their father's appeared to be worried.

'Mr Grant has gone into a meeting with my boss. If you want I will make sure he is still in that meeting or he has left before you go, okay? Why did you say he's a nutter?'

Marcus took a deep breath. 'When he is drunk or when he gets angry, we all keep away from him and that included Alison, her brother and Mrs Grant. He can be very nasty.'

Mr Devonport spoke up. 'Detective Watson, you see the state of our children. Can we take them home now?'

CHAPTER THIRTY-ONE

Watson crawled through the traffic on his way home. A meal, with the family followed by a curl up on the sofa with Sally, watching some trashy TV programme of her choosing with a bottle of wine.

Watson put on Eric Clapton's *Journeyman* CD and whacked up the sound of *No Alibi's* to try and drown out the traffic.

Watson pulled into the driveway of his house and sat as Eric finished the guitar solo on the song *No Alibis*. Very apt for today at work he thought. No alibis and many lies.

As he came through the front door, Sally popped her head out of the living room. 'We have a visitor.' She came out into the hall as Watson took off his jacket and exchanged his shoes for slippers.

'Who?' Watson looked confused.

'Simon's manager from the football team.'

'Nick? He's here?' Watson followed Sally into the living room.

Nick Thomas had been Simon's manager at Rylands for the last two years. Taking the team over when they were in the under twelves. Under his tutelage, they won the second division in his first year. For the last two seasons they had been holding their own in first division. Simon, being the midfield dynamo of the team.

Nick was sat on the sofa with Simon as they came in. He got up and offered the man his hand.

'Nick, this is a surprise,' Watson said, shaking his hand.

'I have some news which I thought I should tell you in person. West Ravenwood Rovers have been looking at the under fourteens league for the last month, sending scouts out to matches. This morning I received a letter from them asking if I could see if two of the team they were interested in, wanted to start training with their team. They are very interested in Simon.'

Simon sat there smiling. Watson looked at him, then Sally, pondering what to say.

'Who am I to stand in the way of the next Paul Pogba or Frank Lampard?'

Simon jumped up and hugged him, then ran around the room like he had scored the winning goal in the cup final with Jason and Rachael joining him.

Watson signed the forms Nick had brought with him while going over training schedule and match dates.

When the manager left, Watson decided that a meal out to celebrate was in order.

CHAPTER THIRTY-TWO

'You said when I came to work for you that you would leave my wife and family alone.' Monteith was furious with the man sat behind the desk in front of him. He stood next to Lex, both of them looking like they had gone three rounds with a heavyweight boxer. Both had cuts and swellings to their faces, bruised knuckles, and torn clothes.

'I did give you my word and I have stuck to it.' Jimmy Russell reclined in his leather-backed chair with his hands forming a triangle against his chin.

'Then what was this arsehole,' Monteith said, pointing at Lex, 'doing outside of my mother- in-law's house while–'

Lex landed a right-handed punch to his face, causing Monteith to stagger sideways. Monteith launched himself at Lex but was caught by Ray and Allan before getting anywhere close.

'Stop!' Jimmy jumped up from his chair and slammed his fist down onto the desk. 'I expect better from my employees. Especially those who I have trusted with more prominent jobs than you both deserve. For behaving like bar-room brawlers you will both be paying for the damage you have caused downstairs.'

Earlier in the day, as Monteith had left his mother-in-law's, he'd seen Lex joining the traffic and driving the boss's Range Rover behind him. He could have stopped at the roadside and had it out with him there and then, but getting called before the courts on a road rage charge was not worth the hassle of losing his job over. He'd kept Lex in his sight, via the rear-view mirror, all the way back to the casino. Monteith parking his BMW at the edge of the main car park. Lex drove behind the casino to park his.

Monteith found Lex in the kitchen, pouring himself a cup of coffee.

'Want one?' Lex asked holding the coffee pot. Monteith nodded out of courtesy.

'Been anywhere good?' Lex asked with a hint of a smile while handing Monteith his coffee.

'Just been to see my wife and kids, but you know that already don't you.'

'I don't know what you mean,' Lex replied, not turning to face him.

As they left the kitchen and made their way towards the doors leading to the casino floor. Lex, in front of him, Monteith grabbed him by his arm and spun him round, spilling both their drinks.

Lex looked at Monteith's hand on his arm with disdain. Looking up and with menace in his eyes, he said, 'I suggest you remove that if you don't want it broken.'

Monteith released it. 'You were parked outside the house while I was there. I saw you as I pulled away.'

Lex leaned into Monteith. 'Well if you saw me, there is no point denying it.'

'Leave my family alone,' Monteith replied almost nose to nose with Lex.

'And if I don't.'

'You don't want to find out.'

Monteith turned to leave.

'I don't know why your wife married a dickhead detective like you; she would have done better marrying me. I would have treated her better.'

Monteith flew at Lex, who retaliated so that in seconds they were punching and kicking each other until they crashed through the double doors and onto the casino floor. Staff scattered out of their way as Lex launched Monteith across one of the tables and into the chairs on the other side. Monteith got up and smashed one of the chairs against Lex's torso causing him to double over. Monteith followed up with a kick to the solar plexus. Monteith grabbed Lex and ran him into the front of a fruit machine. Lex slumped to the floor as the machine toppled over. The security guards broke up the fight.

Now they stood in front of Jimmy Russell.

'Go and get cleaned up, then Keith, you are to stay in the office and don't come out. Lex, just get out of my sight and go home. I've got important guests coming tonight and I don't want you around in the state you are in when they arrive. Now, piss off out of my sight.'

CHAPTER THIRTY-THREE

Monteith went into the cloakroom to change and freshen up. Lex was dumped into a taxi to take him home. Ray would have to drive the boss home later.

A short while later Monteith had settled into watching the CCTV screens while eating his evening meal of steak and ale pie and chips. His face and body ached.

The big rollers wouldn't be in for some time, though he remained vigilant at all times. Monteith heard the door to the security office open behind him.

'You certainly gave Lex as good as he gave you,' Ray said, pulling up a chair to sit.

'Got what he deserved, the wanker,' Monteith replied. Spotting something on a camera, he radioed one of the security officers, 'S O to Bruce, customer at the bar giving Justine some grief. Check it out please.'

'Lex thinks he is something big because he came up from London. Dropped the A off Alex because he thought it made him sound harder,' Ray explained.

Monteith pointed his fork at Ray. 'He ain't hard. You want hard, go and look at some of the nutters in the prisons. Some of the things they have been put away for would give you nightmares.'

'And you gave all that up for sitting in front of a bank of CCTV screens?'

'It was this or end up dead in a ditch somewhere,' Monteith spat.

'Yes, the boss only makes one-sided deals in his favour. That's why we are working for him.' Ray looked at the floor as he was talking.

Monteith turned to face him. 'He had something on you?'

'He has something on most of us. Yours was your gambling, mine well . . .'

He didn't appear to be forthcoming.

'And Lex?'

Ray shrugged. 'All I know is that it had something to do with his time in London.'

Monteith made a mental note to check out both men's histories from before they began working for the Russells.

CHAPTER THIRTY-FOUR

THURSDAY

Roger Young was up bright and early at 6 a.m. By seven he was on the road after he had received a call the previous evening asking for help to put a fence up in a nearby village. Enjoying the scenic view along the back roads, the fields growing crops boarded by a hedgerow. Little villages with stone-built houses and thatched roofs. Chocolate box villages, not these big concrete monstrosities, which gradually ate up the countryside. Here there was no-one to bother him, and no-one to tell him what to do.

Rounding a bend he saw a car broken down at the roadside. He passed it slowly. Sat in the driver's seat was a young woman with her phone to her ear. Young signalled and pulled in front of the car, an Alfa Romeo, stopped and got out.

The woman told him that the car had just died on her, and that she didn't have a strong enough signal on her phone to call her breakdown service or her husband. Young said he could take her to the newsagent's in the next village which would be open at this hour. She could phone from there.

The woman agreed, exited the vehicle, locked the car and followed Young down the passenger side of his van. Opening the door he invited her to step up into the cab. As she turned to climb up and in Young whacked the back of her head with a hammer twice. She collapsed forward against the seat. Young stuffed her into the footwell and covered her with a blanket.

He usually planned these things but sometimes you had to take advantage of a situation.

The fence would have to wait.

-X-

Superintendent Matthews, deciding to sit in on the morning briefing, glowered at everyone.

Wright; fuming after the dressing down she'd just received, gave the smug pompous git daggers.

'Claire Townsend. Emma, you interviewed the husband yesterday?'

'Yes. Stuart Parker, fiancé, not husband. He said that their relationship had been on the rocks for some time. He found Claire had been sleeping with her boss and said she was moving with him to Manchester to work up there. He thought she had done that because he had not heard from or seen her since she'd walked out.'

'Where did she work?'

'At the tyre and exhaust place where her body was found.' Emma announced.

'I want you to find out where the manager of that place went to in Manchester. Did he take over another garage up there?'

'Alison Grant. Where are we with her? Paul, you said to me earlier something about the autopsy?'

Paul Sandall stood to address the room. 'Mac's autopsy found that Alison, like Claire Townsend, died from blunt force trauma to the back of the head. She had ligature marks on her wrists and ankles. But unlike Claire, she'd had intercourse prior to her death as a trace of semen was found. We're awaiting the results of a DNA analysis from that.'

'It could be from Marcus,' Watson interjected. 'They were all out on the town the night before she went missing. We need to ask him if they had sex.'

'Also,' Paul continued, she'd had a chunk of her hair cut off from the back of her head.'

'A trophy!?' Lorimer exclaimed.

'A what?,' Paul looked confused.

'We know how she was killed and where she was dumped but not where she was taken or by who,' Wright cut in.

PC Kendall put his hand up. 'A report I saw from one of the squad cars might shed light on where she was taken. When foot patrol spoke to a Mr Rose, who was in his front garden tending his roses would you believe, he told uniform he often saw Alison running past his house on a Monday. If he was in his garden they would wave hello to one another. But he didn't see her last Monday.'

'Where along the route is Mr Rose's house?' Wright asked.

'About a quarter of a mile from Alison's house.' Kendall got up and approached the map of the area attached to the wall. 'There. His house is the first one of those three.' He pointed to a trio of properties set back from the road, each having large front and back gardens.

'That narrows down our search. Let's get CSI out there.'

CHAPTER THIRTY-FIVE

Within an hour the CSI team were on the ground, starting their search from the railway line at the back of the estate where the Grants lived. Watson and Sandall parked up on the estate where the cut-through led to the unmanned crossing over the tracks which Alison must have used. The cut-through was less than a hundred metres from the Grants' house. Watson looked around, taking in the surroundings. He knew what the houses were like as they were the same as the one he lived in on the south side of the city. Not as well built as the council houses which were put up when West Ravenswood expanded in the seventies but sturdy enough, and with emphasis on providing green spaces and cycle ways for the residents.

'I'd be surprised if she was taken here with all the houses overlooking each other and the road,' Sandall commented.

'If he or she was determined enough to snatch her, an estate like this would not be a deterrent,' Watson replied. 'Off the road snatches are more common than you think.'

As they got to the end of the cut-through, a goods

train trundled past pulling freight containers. The sound was deafening as the clanking and banging of the trucks on the rails made it hard to hear yourself think, never mind talk to someone next to you. And the rush of air almost knocked them sideways before they could grab hold of the railings.

They looked both ways checking there were no more trains coming before crossing to join the CSIs.

'Are we looking for anything in particular?' Sandall asked Watson as they walked up the lane.

'From what we know of Mr Rose's report, Alison may have been snatched between here and Mr Rose's house. Mrs Grant told us she listened to music as she ran. But when Alison was found on the embankment no phone or other personal effects were found. CSI did a good sweep of the area. That means either whoever took her got rid of her phone, which may have been around here, or they still have it.'

Sandall looked at the lane in front of them. CSI were going to have a job finding anything with the amount of things that had been dumped here. Unlike where she'd been found, it was clear the maintenance workers hadn't got as far as clearing this far. Piles of rubbish, building masonry, and some white goods were among the items stashed in the trees. 'A beautiful area like this and those that don't care just come along and ruin it for everyone.'

'The countryside is a beautiful place until you add people,' Watson mused.

They walked along to Mr Rose's house. Glancing in the hedges that bordered the road from the fields. Nothing present stood out among the long grass and thorn ladened hedgerows.

Mr Rose was standing on his driveway talking to his next door neighbour. Watson and Sandall approached, flashing the man their ID cards.

'Looks like they have come for you, Frank. It's been nice knowing you,' The neighbour joked.

'Get off you silly bugger,' Mr Rose said with a chuckle. 'Detectives, what can I do for you?'

'You spoke to our friends in uniform a couple of days ago about the disappearance of a female runner?'

'Yes, have you found her?' Mr Rose asked.

Sandall glanced at Watson wondering what to say. 'Unfortunately we have found her body. We just wanted to go over a couple of things with you, if you don't mind?'

'That's shocking to hear.' Mr Rose shook his head. 'Her parents must be going through hell.'

'You said you saw Alison running most mornings?'

'Was that her name? pretty looking young lady she was. Yes, when I was in the garden. She would wave at me either going on her run or coming back. Didn't stop for a chat though.'

'How busy does this road get around that time in the morning?'

Mr Rose took out a handkerchief and blew his nose before answering. 'Sorry, getting over a cold. Erm just the normal traffic coming out of the village, and farm machinery when the harvest it on.'

'What about vehicles using that dead-end back there?' Sandall asked, pointing over the hedges.

'Fly-tipping alley you mean.' Mr Rose gave a rueful look as he said the words. 'Vans and cars with trailers come and go. Mainly during the early hours or late at night when they think no-one will catch them, bloody nuisance they are.'

'Were there any around the day Alison went missing?' Watson butted in looking at Sandall.

'I was talking to our postman, Dave, out here when a lad in a small car stopped to ask a question.'

Watson looked at Sandall. This was something that was not in the original report.

'What did the lad ask?' Watson quizzed.

'He asked if we had seen a female runner, said he was a friend of hers. We said we hadn't but we would keep an eye out.'

'You don't happen to remember the model or colour of the car, do you?'

'Not the model, but it was silver if that helps.'

Watson thanked him for his help, handed him a card with his direct contact number on, and told him that if he remembered anything else to call him straight away.

Walking back to fly tip alley Watson's phone rang.

Seconds later he turned to Sandall and said, 'CSI have just found a phone with headphones attached to it in the hedge.'

-X-

The Crime Scene Manager handed Watson two plastic evidence bags, one containing the phone and earphones, the other a water bottle. 'They were found in the hedge just over there.' He pointed to his right, where the lane, about thirty yards along from the railway crossing, had been taped off.

Watson looked at the iPhone. Its screen had been broken, a star crack in the middle had radiated out and there were scratches on its back. Watson pressed the *on* button but nothing happened. It was either broken or had run out of battery.

The CSIs resumed their search. Which included being on the lookout for tyre tread marks and cross-referencing them with those found at the railway embankment. They would also check the road surface for dried blood and broken glass, or any flattened weeds for signs of a struggle. Chances were slim any evidence had survived this long but miracles happened.

He took a photo of the bags that had been logged as evidence and ten minutes later Watson and Sandall were sitting beside Joan in the garden. 'We have been searching along the cut-though and by the lane. We've found what we believe to be Alison's phone. We just need you to confirm this.'

Joan burst into tears at the sight of the picture on the screen of his phone. Marcus came over and hugged her from behind. 'Her watch. Have you found her watch?' Joan looked at him, wide-eyed.

'Not while we were there. What type is it?'

'A Fitbit. Keeps track of your heartrate, blood pressure, calculates how many steps you've taken throughout the day, has a timer to measure distance, can even track how many hours of sleep you get and what form it takes.'

'Does it have GPS?' Sandall asked.

'If you are wondering if we can track the watch, I tried that on my searches and came up with nothing. The range is limited.'

'Talking about your searches,' Watson replied to Marcus. 'Did you speak to anyone while you were out looking for Alison?'

'I asked an old bloke if he had seen Alison. He was talking to a postman by his front gate if that's what you are on about. He said he saw her most days but not the day she went missing. I also spoke to a few others but none of them had seen Alison.'

Watson nodded. 'We believe now we have the phone and water bottle that she was snatched before reaching his property. It's looking likely to have been that she was snatched as soon as she crossed the railway line.'

Joan Grant burst into tears again. Watson signalled to Sandall that they should leave.

'Marcus, could you see us out please?'

As they got to the front door Watson turned to Marcus. 'I have one more question, for now. I did not want to embarrass you in front of Mrs Grant with it, you see, but on the Sunday evening when you got back from town with Alison did you have sex?'

'Y- yes, we did,' Marcus replied. 'Why?'

'Just a line of inquiry we're following.'

'Has she been sexually assaulted?' Marcus asked.

'No, there is no evidence to suggest anything like that happened.'

CHAPTER THIRTY-SIX

Roger Young parked his van close to the farmhouse, passenger side nearest the front door. He unlocked the front door, after making sure there were no other vehicles on the road. After taping the woman's legs and hands together and applying a strip to her mouth, he lifted her dead weight onto his shoulder. Blood had pooled in the footwell and it covered part of her face. He whipped in through the door, slammed the car door, locked it and carried her down to her final resting place.

Time was against him as he was late for his latest job, so the photographs and hair cutting would have to wait until later.

-X-

Watson knocked on the door of Monteith's house loudly for the second time and stood back. Looking up he saw the bedroom curtains twitch. He had dropped Sandall off at HQ, instructing him to tell the DCI what they had discovered and to update the whiteboards and databases.

The door opened, revealing Monteith.

'My God, Keith, you look like hell.'

'You should see the other guy.' Monteith left the door open for Watson to enter, and went into the kitchen.

'What the fuck happened to you?' Watson stood leaning against the door frame as Monteith banged the kettle and mugs about, trying to make his first drink of the day though it was close to lunchtime.

'One of the so-called bodyguards Russell has, Lex, tried to see how hard I was and regretted it. Can you make the drinks? I need to find some painkillers for this road drill in my head.'

After taking the drinks into the living room Monteith explained exactly what had happened.

'Sounds like you have made yourself at home with the natives.'

'Monkeys acting like wannabe gorillas.' Monteith snorted his disdain.

'And you come in acting like the alpha male has put Lex's nose out of joint.'

'No, up till now I have behaved myself. Said "yes sir" and "no sir", done what was asked of me.'

'Remember you asked me to check on someone called Tommy Burke?'

'Yes?'

'Ten broken fingers – didn't want to name his attackers.'

'What a surprise,' Monteith passed the kitchen carrying a plate of toast. Licking his fingers, he handed the envelope over to Watson.

'What's in here?' Watson started to open it.

'That is your next task. In there are CCTV photos of Lex and Ray, Allan Russell's bodyguards, henchmen, drivers whatever you want to call them. Lex joined them from London; his father was in the force down there as a detective. Got done for a protection racket and killed himself in prison. Don't know much about Ray, local I think.'

'And this?' Watson held up a CD.

'That is a copy of something that happened in the casino the other night. We caught a lad peddling drugs. Allan Russell and Lex dealt with him. You will find out how at the end.'

'Did you catch the lad's name?'

'Wayne Marsh I think, can't be certain.'

Watson shot a look at Monteith. 'Wayne Marsh?'

'Yes. Why?'

'Because when I was last at Mac's place there was a lad with that name brought in. Was found in the park, possible overdose.'

'Bastards,' Monteith shouted. Looking at Watson he said, 'Lex force-fed him the ecstasy tablets he was trying to sell, it's all on that disc.'

CHAPTER THIRTY-SEVEN

THURSDAY 1.20 p.m.

The black Range Rover Evoke was parked up in one of the visitors' parking spaces outside the council offices. In the back, Jimmy Russell sat, staring straight ahead, at the main door of the building he was expecting Ray to appear from within. He checked his watch, cursed the council office for being the most cumbersome and inept he'd had the tribulation of dealing with.

Finally, Ray appeared from inside the council offices. He walked briskly across the car park, got into the driver's seat, leaned back and handed Jimmy a note.

Jimmy took one look at it.

'Drive me back to the casino, we have work to do.'

-X-

Watson arrived back in the office just after 2 p.m. DCI Wright asked him to join her in her office. Already in there were French and Lorimer. Watson unlocked the bottom drawer and took out the envelope Joseph Clayton had given him. He added it to the envelope Monteith had just handed him and walked into the boss's office.

'Terry, Emma, and Karl are not going to be here for the next couple of days,' Wright announced even before he had sat down.

'That's going to leave us a bit thin on the ground.'

'I know but it can't be helped. The National Tyre Company sent us through the employee list for their garage in Copeland. The manager, Nigel Prior, transferred to a garage in Salford, in Greater Manchester, just after it closed. Matthews has just signed off on them going up there to interview him. Contact has been made with the county force up there so they know our presence.'

'That only leaves me, Sandall and PC Kendall. Assuming we still have Kendall?'

'Yes, we still have Kendall. Emma, Karl, you two get off and pack. The accommodation has been organised at a local Premier Inn for this evening. You have a room each. They've been made aware you may arrive late.'

'Oh boss, you spoilsport.' Lorimer pretended to be disappointed. French punched him in the arm.

'It's bad enough I have to share a car with you. You think I was going to share a room as well?' Kendall replied with a smile, before standing and following him out the door.

Watson looked at Wright with curiosity.

'You not noticed the spark between the two of them?'

'You're letting them go to Manchester together. They will either come back married or dead.'

'Just as long as the one still living brings back Nigel Prior,' Wright said. She got out of her chair behind the desk and moved to sit in the one next to Watson. Watson divulged his theory that Alison had disturbed someone fly-tipping something they wanted to be kept out of sight and killed to shut her up.

'Wrong place, wrong time. That's a huge leap you're suggesting?' Wright said unbelievingly.

'It's a long shot, I know, but must be considered. There's nothing to forensically link Alison's murderer to Claire's. The other is that whoever murdered her knew her route, when she would be running, that she'd be alone and that hardly anybody would be around.'

The look on DCI Wright's face suggested she thought the same.

'What do you have in those?' Wright pointed at the envelopes Watson had put down on the coffee table.

'I went to check on Monteith earlier. He was looking rather the worse for wear. Got in a fight yesterday.'

'He hasn't been found out?' Wright looked worried.

'No.' Watson opened the envelope Monteith had given him. 'Looks like he is bearing fruit.' He handed the two photos across to Wright. 'These two are Allan Russell's go-to guys. The ones who dumped Monteith after his abduction. Their names are Lex and Ray. Keith put what he knows about them on the backs of the photos. He's made a good connection with Ray who told him that the Russells have something against each of them tucked away on file but did not go into details about what those things are. Lex is the hard man and the one he had a fight with.'

Wright glanced over to where Kendall sat at his desk typing away. She knocked on the partition window and gestured for him to come over.

'Can you run a facial recognition on these two. Check their backgrounds and see if they have any convictions?'

'Yes, boss.'

Watson continued. 'This disc shows what Lex is capable of.' Wright took the disc and put it into her computer. They watched as the CCTV pictures Monteith had pieced together told the story.

'This Lex guy is an evil bastard,' Wright said. 'Who's the suit he spoke to before leaving the casino?'

'Keith said it was Allan Russell.'

'So we can get both Allan Russell and Lex for . . . What happened to the man?'

'Murder? The lad they force-fed the tablets to was found dead in the park. Mac has his body at his place. The autopsy suggested a drugs overdose, which we now know was not accidental.'

'Him upstairs won't want us to go in and arrest them with Keith still being there though, so we'll have to hang till a while longer. Besides, we'd have to disclose the CCTV images to them during their interview and they'd know where they came from, which would put Keith in danger. I'll update Matthews.'

Watson handed Wright the envelope he'd been given from Clayton. 'You had better give him this too.'

As they were winding up, Sandall knocked on the door and stuck his head in. 'Sorry to bother you. Report has come in, we have another missing woman. About a mile from where Alison Grant went missing.'

CHAPTER THIRTY-EIGHT

Jimmy Russell sat in the leather upholstered chair behind his large oak desk, swirling the scotch round his crystal tumbler. He was surrounded by every bit of refinery money could buy with the two most gormless fuckwits in his employ. Fighting unless sanctioned by him, especially between two of his most trusted employees was a sackable offence. He got up and stood in front of Lex and Monteith.

'You two are disappointments. If it was anyone else who behaved like you did, they'd be lying in hospital beds with feeding tubes down their throats after I'd finished with them. You two are on a final warning; any more sparring and you will be, understood?'

'Yes, boss,' they both responded at the same time.

'Now piss off to either end of the casino and keep out of each other's way until tonight. I have a job for you to do later. Thanks to another numbskull not doing his properly, a visit is needed.'

Jimmy handed Ray a piece of paper. 'You know what to do?' Ray nodded.

'Now get the hell out of my sight!'

-X-

Déjà vu hit Watson and Sandall as they hit the back road, outside a nearby village in search of another missing woman. This time they had a little bit more to go on.

They had been let through the police cordon which had been set up at the end of the road leading out of the village of Little Beck, blocking the route for police to forensically search the area while the traffic had been diverted.

Parking up, they could see an Alfa Romeo had been covered with a forensic tent and a smaller one had been erected close by. They signed the register of attendance before making their way across to a couple of squad cars.

'Afternoon, detectives,' PC Andrew Murray introduced himself, as he stood to one side.

'What have we got?' Watson asked, looking around at the ongoing scene.

We have in the back of the squad car, Mr Craig Field, husband of the missing woman. The car is his wife, Samantha's. He got a call at his workplace at about twelve o'clock from hers asking if she was ill or something. He said he had left work an hour away after he could not reach her on her phone. He came home, found no sign of her, so he started driving around and found her car abandoned here. He has given us a description of Samantha, her age, height, weight, and a photo. We have informed the station so other uniforms can look out for her.

Watson and Sandall thanked the officer and approached the squad car.

'You can take this, Paul.' Watson encouraged.

Sandall slid in next to the husband.

'Mr Field? My name is DC Sandall and this is DI

Watson.' Craig Field nodded and said. 'Hello,' weakly. He'd been crying and was in an agitated state. He was playing with his phone, still trying to dial Samantha's number in the vain hope that she would answer.

'Mr Field, we have been told that your wife's description has been circulated across the media and we are looking out for her,' Sandall said.

Craig nodded.

'Is there anything else you can tell us which may help us to locate your wife? Anywhere she might have gone? A friend she's close to who she might have visited?'

Craig shook his head. 'No, she was spending the day in the office.'

'How were things between you two?'

'Our marriage was fine, just celebrated our second anniversary last week. Spent last weekend away, at a hotel,' he replied, getting out of the car.

The Crime Scene Manager came over and pulled Watson aside. 'We've taken external fingerprints and skin cell fragment samples from the car door handle, to compare against Mr Field's. We need to look inside but its all locked up. Can you witness us if we have to break the window?'

'One moment.' He strode back to the patrol car and leaned in to the open passenger door to speak to Mr Field. 'You don't by any chance have a spare key to your wife's car?' Watson asked.

'Actually I do,' Mr Field replied. 'We have one for each other's in case we lose them.' Field handed it to Watson.

'Shit!' Craig Field said alarmingly.

'What is it?' Watson asked.

'I had completely forgotten. We had a motion activated dash-cam fitted to Sam's car three months ago when the insurance needed renewing. Got a discount for having one.'

A Crime Scene Investigator opened up the car with her gloved hand and checked the footwell for where it looked like the camera had fallen from the circular smear on the window where it had obviously been held.

Retrieving it he said, 'We may have a recording of what happened to Samantha.'

CHAPTER THIRTY-NINE

'And where did Watson say he got this from?' Superintendent Matthews spoke from behind his desk, in his top-floor office as he looked again at the two sheets of A4 paper in his hands. Specifically two lines halfway down the second sheet.

'From Joseph Clayton,' DCI Wright replied. 'Clayton said it was his security; these are copies of the original which he has stashed somewhere.'

'Has Watson seen this?'

'No. I think he would have said something about the contents of the documents if he had, especially after what we have just read. Joseph Clayton is a reliable source, Guv. He's helped the agency in the past.'

'The information helps the Claytons in what they are doing. I'm not that wet behind the ears sitting up here.'

'Where is Watson now?'

'Dealing with that missing woman, out at Little Beck. Both him and DC Sandall should be back soon,' Wright said, looking at her watch.

'When he comes in, bring him up here. This stays between these four walls until we can confirm or counter any of what's written here.'

'Of course. Can I have some more manpower to do the checks on the smaller pieces of info that's been given us? PC Kendall is already looking into Allan Russell's cronies, and with Lorimer and French in Manchester, we are a bit stretched.'

'I will see what I can do.'

-X-

Watson and Sandall left Little Beck just after 4.30 p.m. They had seen uniform drive off, escorting Craig Field in his car back to his house. The CSI were packing up. The dash-cam footage was wending its way across town to be viewed. Samantha Field's car was being loaded onto a lorry to be brought to one of the force's own garage for a forensic examination.

'Why are we here again? I thought CSI had gone over this before?' Sandall asked Watson as he pulled up next to fly tip alley.

'If things don't feel right they're not?'

Looking confused Sandall followed Watson from the car and towards the hedgerow.

Watson crouched and pulled away some fencing that had been tossed onto the ground. 'When we were at the Grants', I noticed for some reason that they'd had part of their fencing replaced, and it looked quite recent. I remembered, because they looked the same as these panels here. Now what if the person who fixed the fence was the one who took Alison? He came along here and dumped these, spotted her . . . Or, having seen her passing by, chose here to dump these broken panels off at the same time as snatching her?' He saw the frown on Sandall's face and lowered his gaze.

'Is there a manufacturers name on these panels?'

Sandall asked.

Watson turned one round, and spotted the faint etching on one of the pieces below. 'Roger Young.'

CHAPTER FORTY

Roger Young unlocked the door to his prize. He had been visualising her throughout his working day. Her hair, her smell and the pictures he would take to join his collection. Her hair, a piece of which would end up in a little plastic box on the shelf.

The boss at the site he had been working had been a pain in the arse, always nitpicking his work. This was wrong, that was wrong. The fence posts were the wrong type and put in the wrong place. He wanted to stick one of the posts right where the sun didn't shine by the end of the day.

Opening the door, she was still where he had laid her, on the mattress. She had moved slightly possibly through drifting in and out of consciousness. At the moment she was still.

He removed his camera from out of its case and started taking photographs of her. He didn't know her name; this had been an instinctive one. The ones before had been planned, so he'd known most of them. He finished snapping photos and picked up the large pair of scissors. Finding a chunk of hair which had not been polluted with blood he removed it with precision. Taking it over to his desk he held it to his nose to sniff her unique fragrance.

After selecting a good number of strands he put them into one of his small plastic boxes and wrote on the front the date and where she'd been found. Satisfied, he placed the box on the shelving alongside the others. Opening a draw he put the rest of the hair along with what he had already collected. He would start on the next phase tonight.

-X-

Watson was seated next to DCI Wright outside Superintendent Matthews' office. His Personal Assistant, Beryl, was packing away for the evening and had given them stern looks as they had entered, as if to say 'what are you doing here, don't you know the time'.

Matthews opened his door and beckoned them in, saying goodnight to Beryl at the same time. As they sat down Matthews took his phone off the receiver, indicating that he didn't want us to be disturbed.

'Did DCI Wright tell you why I wanted to see you?' Matthews started.

'Only that it had something to do with what Joseph Clayton had given to me.' Watson was still unsure what was going on. He had been summoned into Wright's office as soon as he and Sandall had got back to HQ. There hadn't been enough time for Sandall to update him on what had been found.

'What exactly were Joseph Clayton's words when he handed you the envelope?' Matthews asked in a measured tone.

'He said: If we were looking to take down the Russells, what's in there would help us. In that envelope are photocopies of a book he has stashed away as insurance.'

'And you have not looked at it prior to this evening?'

'No, Why? What was in it?'

Matthews opened a file on his desk and removed two sheets of paper. He leaned over the desk handing them to Watson. 'The second sheet halfway down, it's marked.'

Watson glanced at the first sheet, then looked closer at the second one, mouthing the words silently to himself trying to take in what he was reading. He shot a look of shock at Matthews then at Wright. 'You're kidding, right? This is a joke?' Watson looked dumbstruck.

'Did you know about this?' Matthews asked Watson.

'No.'

'Do you think he knows about it?'

'If he does he has not mentioned it to me. Does this change the operation?' Watson said in a worried tone.

'No, it doesn't, but we may need to pull the plug on this earlier than planned due to the level of risk this poses.'

Watson and Wright left the office looking like they had found a tenner that had turned out to be fake. As they entered the main office Sandall and PC Kendall were on their phones. Sandall signalled to them both to join him.

'That was CSI. They have viewed that dashcam footage and according to what has been discovered we have dynamite.'

CHAPTER FORTY-ONE

An hour later the full force of West Ravensthorpe police service was poised outside Roger Young's farm. Armed Response Unit officers were accompanied by Watson, Sandall, Wright and PC Kendall. An ambulance was parked nearby. DCI Wright was talking to the head of the ARU to ascertain the best way to breach the farmhouse. Young's van was parked close to the house and could be used as cover.

Watson could feel a massive headache coming on and the thought of a long night working into the early hours of the morning was only exemplifying it.

After coming out of Matthews' office, and before seeing the video in CSI, he had taken a bathroom break to get his mind around what he had just read:

Keith Monteith is half-brother to Jimmy and Allan Russell.

He stared at the washed-out face in the mirror. Stress lines had appeared to highlight his features. His eyes were heavy. His hair looked greyer.

'They make you look distinguished,' Sally had told

him.

'No, I'm getting old,' He'd replied, grumpily.

Wright returned from her chat with the ARU coordinator.

'We are going in. Checks have been completed to the barn over there, which was clear, and the van. Blood had been found underneath the passenger side door. That means hopefully he has Samantha Field in there with him. Get ready.'

As quickly and as quietly as twenty-odd uniformed and armed police could go, they surrounded the front of the farmhouse. Wright, Watson, and Sandall stood back until the front door had been forced open with a battering ram.

'Armed police! Stay where you are!'

A small army of helmeted and vested men and women stormed through the gap where the front door had been seconds before, to secure the area. Roger Young was in the kitchen sitting at the table. He was brought to the ground and cuffed while officers split up to search the house, taking the stairs three at a time and bolting through the doors of each downstairs room. Footsteps bounded above them, followed by shouts of 'Clear!'

Wright, Watson, and Sandall entered the kitchen.

'Where is Samantha Field, Mr Young?' Wright demanded.

'Who?' Young snarled back, but Watson spotted a quick flick of his eyes towards the door under the staircase.

'Boss,' he said, pointing to it. 'Where's the key?' Watson yelled.

Sandall grabbed a bunch that were on the table and lobbed them to Watson. Three tries later they were in. Watson leading the charge down the stairs, while Wright managed to find the light switch. They stopped dead as the lights came on. The walls were covered with photographs of bound, gagged and terrified women.

'Watson!' Wright pointed to a door inside the basement, causing him to turn around.

Fiddling with the keys he managed to get the one that fit, slotted it into the lock and shoved the door wide.

'Get paramedics in here now! he bellowed, as Wright joined him in the room.

In the corner was Samantha Field, tied and bound, lying on a soiled mattress. Wright held Watson back from doing anything, as she quite rightly reminded him that this was a crime scene and nothing should be touched. The paramedics pushed their way into the room and rushed towards Samantha.

'She's alive,' one of them called out, as the other – gloved and ready to hand the bindings to the police to bag as evidence – started removing the ties around her wrists and feet, and the tape across her mouth. She didn't respond when asked if she could hear them. 'We need to move her fast.'

Watson turned to exit the basement, hurriedly. Wright grabbed his arm. 'Terry, we've got him bang to rights and we have saved her.'

'He does not deserve any rights,' Watson said through gritted teeth.

'I know he doesn't but let's be professional here. We don't want to give the CPS a reason to question our behaviour.'

They both came back up to the kitchen just as DCI Wright was reading him his rights.

'Get him out of here!' Watson added when she had finished.

The paramedics left soon after with Samantha, the ambulance wailing, blue lights spinning. A very stretched CSI service team arrived and had already begun to tape off and photograph the land surrounding the property as well as Young's van.

'How many do you think he's taken?' Sandall asked.

'Well, there were at least ten women pictured in the photographs on those walls,' Wright replied with a sigh.

'Including Alison Grant!' Watson exclaimed.

In the car on the drive back to the headquarters Wright spoke to their reflections in the rear-view mirror. 'I want you two to go home when we get back. Young is not going anywhere and we have twenty-four hours to charge him, which we will do. I want you bright-eyed and bushy-tailed in that interview room.'

CHAPTER FORTY-TWO

'Don, Don, someone's in the house. Don, wake up!'

Angela Spedding was in bed, shaking with fear while trying to shake her husband awake. She turned her bedside light on.

'What the bloody hell are you doing?' Don rolled away from Angela, getting caught in the duvet and taking it with him, uncovering her in the process.

'Don. I heard something downstairs.' She shook him again on his shoulder making sure he stayed awake.

'What you doing woman!' Don turned back, squinting against the light, his hairy chest visible above the duvet.

'Haven't you heard a word I have been saying? There is someone in the house.' Angela was practically climbing the headboard.

'It's your imagination; you should stop reading those Tony Forder crime books before coming to bed. It's doing your head in,' Don said, before the sound of something crashing downstairs changed his mind.

'I told you,' Angela whisper-yelled.

'Shut up woman.' Don threw back the duvet and reached behind the wardrobe for the baseball bat he kept. 'Stay there,' he said, creeping around the bed to the door. Opening it slightly he took a peek out onto the landing. Not seeing anything, he opened the door wider and checked further round to the stairs. At the bottom, the fragments of a glass vase was lying on the floor, the flowers scattered over a pool of water.

Don descended the stairs stealthily. Reaching the bottom he maneuvered around the broken glass, opened the front room door and switched on the light to find it had been ransacked. He stepped further in, baseball bat raised, but the intruder, who was behind the door, whacked Don over the head with a cosh. Don dropped the bat and grabbed at his head, and in doing so stumbled and fell to the ground. The intruder hit him again, sending him into darkness.

Angela was by this time near the bottom of the stairs and started to scream after seeing what had happened to Don. The intruder turned and looked at her. His accomplice came out of the kitchen. Both were wearing balaclavas and were dressed all in black. Angela shrieked again and ran back upstairs into the bedroom and tried to lock the door. The intruders both bolted up the stairs after her, pushing the door open as she ran to the window and opened the curtains, shouting for help, hoping someone would hear her. She found herself flying back onto the bed looking up as one of the intruders closed the curtains.

'What the fuck are you doing?' Monteith shouted through his balaclava at Lex.

'Just making sure the message was received,' Lex said, looking at Angela Spedding as he approached the bed.

'I'm out of here; we've done what we needed to do,' Monteith said, moving for the door.

'Getting scared are we?' Lex started to laugh.

'Piss off.' Monteith left and ran down the stairs. He didn't want to be here but he'd been given no choice. Reaching the bottom stair he checked on Don Spedding, he was still out cold. He heard the man's wife's shrill as he made his way out of the back door and onto the narrow lane backing the house.

'He's fucking off his head!' Monteith said, jumping into the back of the Range Rover Evoke.

'Where's Lex?' Ray asked from the driver's seat.

'According to him, making sure the message was received by doing whatever he is doing to Spedding's wife.' Monteith was fuming. He knew there was a chance he could get dragged into Allan Russell's dealings every so often, but issuing beatings was not on that list.

'He's starting to get to be a liability,' Ray said, staring out of the windscreen, looking out Lex's large frame. 'There have been a few times he has gone over the top when we were out on business.'

Monteith was just about to press Ray on what he'd said when Lex came lumbering out of the shadows, jumped into the front of the car and Ray pulled out of their hiding place.

'That was fun.' Lex grinned while taking off his balaclava.

'Tell me she is still alive?' Ray spat the question out.

'Course she is.' Looking back at Monteith, 'What did this wimp tell you? I was killing her?' Lex laughed. 'She passed out after I slapped her a couple of times.'

'And Don?'

'He'll wake up with a headache. Now let's get back and have a drink.'

Monteith sat quietly in the back seat.

I've had enough.

CHAPTER FORTY-THREE

Watson collapsed into his chair in the living room. It had been a long and busy day. It wasn't until he'd got home that he realised a shop bought ham and cheese sandwich and a Mars bar was all he had eaten since he had left the house that morning.

Sally had admonished him for that, then made a large spaghetti bolognese with garlic bread while he took a shower. Over the meal, they talked about their days. Without going into detail, Watson told Sally what had happened as the kids came in and out of the kitchen. Jason and Simon were old enough to know what daddy did for a living, but Rachael was still far too young to understand.

Simon was still on cloud nine after being asked to train with West Ravenswood Rovers. He was going to get the training and playing kits at the weekend. He had also been promised new boots.

With all the kids in bed, Sally brought in a can of John Smiths for Watson and a bottle of wine for herself before plonking herself down on the sofa beside him.

'What's up Inspector?' Sally asked.

'Just tired is all,' he replied, tapping the bottom of

the can then pulling the ring top before taking a long and much-needed swig.

'You can't kid me, we've been married too long,' Sally said, filling her glass with red wine.

Watson sighed. 'You know that envelope that Joseph Clayton gave me?'

Sally nodded. 'Yes.'

'Well, I gave it to DCI Wright and she and Matthews opened it.' Watson took another swig of beer. 'I got called into the super's office when I got back from Little Beck.'

Sally could see he was struggling with how to continue. She got up and sat on the floor between his legs, on her knees, placing her drink on the nearby table. 'What was in the envelope?'

'Joseph came up trumps with what he gave us, we just have to corroborate it.'

'So what's the problem?'

'If what we read about a certain member of the force is correct, mentioning no names, things could get tricky at work.'

Sally didn't press him.

'Okay, Inspector, if you follow me upstairs I can take your mind off work and put it to something far more pleasurable,' Sally said, standing, with a glint in her eyes.

CHAPTER FORTY-FOUR

FRIDAY 7.30 a.m.

The smell of bacon and sausage baps hit the nasal cavities of Watson, Sandall and Kendall as the three of them entered the office. DCI Wright and Superintendent Matthews were sitting eating.

'Don't stand on ceremony, lads,' Matthews said, as they entered the incident room. 'There's plenty to go round. We have a big day in front of us and I thought a hearty breakfast would be in order.' The three of them looked at one another, rendered speechless.

'Get over here or we will eat the lot,' Wright advised, before they rushed across the room to the table of food.

'Lorimer and French are not going to like that they have been left out of this,' Sandall spoke through a mouthful of bacon and bread.

'Lorimer and French are not here. Anyway, Frenchie is a vegetarian,' Watson corrected him.

'Bet she got some sausage last night,' Wright blurted. Everyone stopped eating and looked at her, her face turning scarlet, before the room exploded in laughter. While devouring the baps, talk turned to more pressing things.

'I have been told that Roger Young had a visit from

an on-call solicitor last night and she will be coming back in an hour. Do we have all our facts in order for we interview him?'

Wright picked up two files and handed them to Watson and Sandall.

'In there you will find the details of what CSI found on Samantha Field's car, fingerprints etc. As well as what we've ascertained of her abduction from the dash cam footage. That is just for starters. Prelim report from Young's van found Samantha's blood on the passenger side footwell as well as on a hammer and a blanket found within the vehicle. So we've got enough evidence to charge him with abduction, GBH and false imprisonment to start with.'

'How is Samantha? Is there an update on her condition?' Watson asked.

'Had a call at seven this morning from PC Walker who has been guarding her overnight. Samantha is on life support after having an operation to remove a blood clot on her brain. Skull fractured in three places. Doctors say it is still too early to say if she will survive due to the length of time she is likely to have spent unconscious and without medical attention.'

'Anything from CSI regarding Alison Grant? We know she was there because he had photographed her in his house and tacked it to the wall within the property, alongside the others.'

'Not yet. Kendall, have you finished collecting the information on Lex and Ray?'

'Yes, boss.'

Okay, can you start looking at the reports of missing women locally, and see which ones match the photographs on Young's wall? We need to make a start on that this morning.'

'Yes, boss.'

DCI Wright checked the time. It was 8.15 a.m.

'Okay, Watson and Sandall you go ahead and interview Young. I think you're in room three. Kendall, come with me and give me an update on Lex and Ray.'

As Kendall and Wright headed into her office, Matthews followed Watson and Sandall out into the incident room.

-X-

The lounge curtains were still closed at 8 a.m. as the postman pushed the envelopes through the letterbox. Nothing stirred from within the house. Monteith did not move from his seat, where he continued to replay the incident he had taken part in several hours before.

Things have got out of hand. I'm out of my depth.

Monteith stared out of the window at the sunshine as it filtered through the crack between the curtains. He picked up his phone and, finding Watson's number in his list of *contacts*, he hesitated before sending him a text message that read:

Need to get out of this now!

CHAPTER FORTY-FIVE

TUESDAY 9.a.m.

Roger Young had been brought up from the cells and had been put into interview room three. His solicitor was waiting for him. Watson and Sandall gave them ten minutes before starting the interview process. Watson took one last look at his phone before going in and spotted Monteith's text.

'Just a moment Paul, I need to make a call. Let them sweat a couple more minutes.' Watson nipped down the corridor and dialled Monteith.

''Bout time you called.'

Monteith's opening salvo took Watson by surprise.

'I'm just about to go into an interview, what's so urgent?'

'I helped in a visit last night on behalf of the Russells.'

'What?' Watson was not sure he'd heard that properly.

'I was told I had to go on a visit with Lex and Ray to someone who had pissed off the Russells,' Monteith said in a slow monotone voice.

Sandall had been joined by DCI Wright and was looking at Watson.

'Okay. I need to get into this interview. Can you

make it in here without Allan Russell's contacts knowing where you are going?' Watson said, smiling at his boss.

'I will try, but I will tell you now, I want out.'

Watson put his phone back into his pocket and returned to Sandall.

'Anything we should be aware of?' Wright asked.

'Monteith. He's coming in.'

Wright thought a moment. 'You two go and interview Young. I'll talk to Monteith when he gets in.'

Watson entered the interview room with Sandall. Both pulled their chairs out opposite Young and his solicitor. Sandall informed both the interview was being audio and visually recorded. They each introduced themselves then Watson reminded Young that he was still under caution.

'Mr Young, can you tell me what your movements yesterday were, say from 7.30 a.m. to 5 p.m?'

Young turned to his solicitor who nodded his assent for him to respond.

'I was at work.'

'And where was that and what do you do for work?'

'I am a fencer and was working over at a new build over at Big Beck.'

'And you were there all day?'

'Yes.'

'And if we spoke to the site foreman there, they can vouch for you?'

'Yes.'

'Mr Young, on your way to work do you remember seeing an Alfa Romeo broken down on the road between Little Beck and Big Beck?'

Young thought. 'Yes. The driver was on the phone so I drove past.'

'You went past? Did you not stop?'

'No.'

'For the record, I am showing Mr Young and his solicitor evidence record RY1 and RY2.' Watson opened the file and removed two evidence bags containing photographs, which he placed on the table in front of Roger Young. His solicitor leaned forward to take a closer look at them and went to ask a question. Watson put his hand up and continued.

'These photographs have been taken from the broken down Alfa Romeo's dash cam recording. The Alfa Romeo that you just told me that you drove past, not stopping to assist the driver who'd broken down. Is that your work van in both of these pictures?' Watson looked Young straight in the eyes.

'No comment,' Young replied.

'Is that your van parked up in front of the Alfa?'

'No comment.'

Watson brought out of the file two more pictures. 'Mr Young is that you getting out of your van and coming towards the driver's side door of the Alfa Romeo?'

The solicitor took one look at the pictures and stopped Young from answering.

'Can I have some time with my client detective, please?'

Sandall said, 'Interview suspended,' and stopped the recording.

Watson turned before leaving. 'Just to let you know we have enough to charge Mr Young for the abduction of the driver of the Alfa Romeo. It's the other nine women who he has pictures of that we want information on.' With that Watson and Sandall left the room leaving a PC standing guard.

They met up with Wright in the corridor. 'Interesting but not surprising that he switched to "no comment" after you'd shown him the photos,' Wright pointed out.

'I expected nothing less. He's not going anywhere and he knows it. He just wants to drag his soles for as long as he can,' Watson said. 'I suggest we see if CSI has come through with anything else that we can get him on before we begin reinterviewing him.'

The three of them made their way back upstairs to the main office. Kendall, who was holding fort, turned from his computer as they entered the incident room.

'Just heard from Lorimer and French, about ten minutes ago. They went to talk to Nigel Prior and he just caved in and admitted to killing Claire Townsend. They have arrested him and are arranging for transport to bring him back down here for an interview.'

'Well, that's at least some good news today.' Wright smiled weakly.

'Have CSI come back with anything else on the other women?' Sandall asked Kendall, as he tucked into a cold bacon bap.

'Funny you should say that.' Kendall picked up a report from his desk. 'Fingerprints on Alison Grant's water bottle and phone match Young's, blood and hair found on a mattress inside Young's van also match Alison's DNA. They are looking at the mattress from the house but there are a lot of bodily fluids, skin cell fragments and hair samples, so it may take a while to distinguish one profile from another.'

'Well, that's two he's going down for.' Watson punched the air.

'We have to get it past the CPS first.' Wright reminded everyone. 'They're going to call me in an hour to go over what we have got.'

Kendall continued. 'I have been cross-referencing missing persons against the pictures found on

Young's wall, which I may add was difficult to look at. I think I have managed to match four of the women from facial analysis, though without DNA samples from CSI it's impossible to be certain.'

'Having to go and speak to the families of these women to tell them we may have an idea of what happened to their loved ones is not something I'm looking forward to,' Watson said.' He read the first name: Viv Miller. 'We cannot even give them rest without a body and that animal down there is the only person who knows where the bodies are.'

Watson glanced at the second name on the list. Caroline Dicks.

One of the phones rang. Sandall, being the closest, picked it up.

Sandall put the phone down. 'Boss, DS Monteith is downstairs.' As soon as he had said it the phone rang again.

'Good, I will see what happened last night to Monteith.' Wright passed Kendall and walked to the door with Watson.

Sandall put the phone back down. 'Boss. That was the hospital. Samantha Field died twenty minutes ago.

CHAPTER FORTY-SIX

Wright looked across her desk at the husk of a man seated on the other side. A man who over the last few months had been abducted, beaten, put in an impossible position by her boss and the biggest crook in West Ravenswood. On top of that his wife had left him, he'd had a fight with one of Allan Russell's henchmen, and had been involved in the enforcement of someone who'd dissed the Russells.

'Surely we have enough on them now to bring them down.' Monteith sounded frustrated.

'We do, but nothing that implicates the Russells exclusively. We don't want them to walk as soon as we have them. Most of what we have relates to both Lex and Ray, and unfortunately now you. But that bridge we can cross later. We can charge Lex and Ray but we need something concrete that we can nail to the brothers. What you have found out is great and we can work with it. Just hang in there a few more days. Will either Lex or Ray help us if we offer them something?'

Monteith thought. 'Ray might, but it depends what the offer is. Lex won't. He is becoming a bit of a liability for the Russells. They ask him to do something and he ends up doing that and a bit more, then he goes over the top. It's like he feels he can do what he wants under their protection.'

Wright pushed her chair back. 'PC Kendall has been doing a little digging into both Lex and Ray's background; let's see what he has found out. They joined Kendall back at his desk. He dug around and found the file.

'Alex John Sullivan – born London, son of DI Peter Sullivan of the Met Police who was arrested for allegedly running a protection racket with five other detectives. Taking a cut from drug dealers who were in their area. Any drugs busts and a small amount of money would go missing. He denied everything and said he was being set up. Hung himself in his cell. Little Alex rebelled and got involved in gangs and petty things. A couple of minor stints in jail, until he assaulted a policeman with a hammer. Served five years of a ten-year stretch, then disappeared from London.

Raymond Lucas, local. Went to the same school as the Russells. Joined the Army but didn't finish the training. The talk was that something happened during training, but getting information off the Army is nigh on impossible. Started a security business for nightclubs, which he sold. Started working for the Russells soon after, mainly as their driver.

There were rumours that a big name in the drug trade died at one of the clubs Ray looked after, but those who were interviewed said they didn't see anything. The case is still open.

'Ray said he knew that the Russells had something on their employees. Maybe this is his.' Monteith mused. Could this be a way to bring Ray onto his side? Lex is a load of dynamite waiting to go off and it could be soon. Ray, on the other hand, plays his cards close to his chest.

-X-

The large metal gates opened and Ray nudged the Range Rover Evoke through and carried on up the drive to the house, parking in front of the main door. Allan Russell and Ray alighted the transport and entered through the door. The grand opulence of Jimmy Russell extended into his home, with fine art and furniture spread throughout the large open-plan house.

Allan and Ray made their way through to the vast kitchen-diner which covered the back of the house, overlooking a manicured lawn which led down to the river, where boats could be moored. A pair of swans passed by, gracefully, while a moorhen bobbed along, looking for food.

'I think this is my best purchase, this house.' Jimmy was standing, dressed in his suit without the jacket, looking out of the bi-folding doors at the garden and the river beyond. Both Allan and Ray joined him, taking in the grandeur of it all. The dulcet tones of Joe Bonamassa's *India/Mountain Time* seeped into the air through the inbuilt Bluetooth wall speakers. Jimmy turned to face the other two.

'Right, what the bloody hell happened last night?' He stared hard at them both as they looked at each other.

'Well?' Jimmy pushed past them and refilled his coffee cup, turning back to Allan and Ray, who stood there looking like two fish moving their mouths with nothing coming out but air.

'My source at the hospital told me that Don Spedding was admitted to A&E early this morning with a head injury. His wife was hysterical. And, the police were there, waiting to interview him.'

'It was Lex,' Ray spat.

'What was Lex? All I said was to give Spedding a warning by leaving the photographs of him and his mistress in the house for his wife to find. What the fuck did Lex do?'

'Spedding came down when they were putting the photos on display. Lex hit him in order to get away.'

'Why didn't Monteith do anything?' Jimmy was getting angry.

'He was in the kitchen so he didn't see it, only heard it,' Ray said, while he and Allan sat down at the kitchen island. 'He did follow Lex upstairs when Spedding's wife came down and saw what had happened. Lex was going to give her a going over before Monteith intervened.'

'Where is super copper by the way?' Jimmy asked, while looking at his watch. Allan took his phone out and dialled through to Monteith.

'Jimmy we need to do something about Lex, he's starting to become a liability,' Ray said, leaning in close to his boss.

'Yes, I'm beginning to think that,' Jimmy sighed.

Allan came off the phone. 'Monteith is on his way to the casino. He's pissed off with Lex after last night. Said Lex went mental while doing a job on Spedding, and he chased his wife upstairs and was going to beat her until he shouted at him to stop.'

Ray looked again at Jimmy. 'I know, I know!' Jimmy said tersely, before walking back towards the open bi-folding doors, coffee cup in hand, with a look that Allan and Ray had seen one too many times before. The look that said he was deciding how best to get rid of Lex.

'What did I miss?' Allan looked confused.

'We were just about to discuss the liability that is

Lex.' Ray updated him.

'Oh! And what I just relayed from Monteith did not help,' Allan said, looking at Jimmy.

'It might have, depends on what Jimmy has planned for him.'

-X-

Monteith knew he did not have a great deal of time. Getting to the casino quickly was a priority after the phone call from Allan. A least he knew where everyone was, except for Lex.

Parking round the back he entered the casino via the staff entrance. Trying to act as normal as he could, saying hello and good morning to the staff already there. Taking a mug of coffee from the kitchen he went into the casino proper. Cleaners were busy tidying, and the bar staff were restocking the shelves. The other security staff did not come in till later in the afternoon so Monteith knew he did not have them to deal with for a while. Lex was nowhere to be found.

Taking the lift up to the floor where the offices were, Monteith worked out that he had limited time before the Russells and Ray came back. Monteith started searching for where the employees' files were kept. The Russells still had to abide by employment law, which included record-keeping. He decided that the only place the files would be kept were in the Russells' own office. Jimmy's to be precise. But how he was going to gain access to search the man's sanctum without arousing suspicion, he did not know.

CHAPTER FORTY-SEVEN

Watson and Sandall exited the interview room. Catching and bringing in culprits, Watson believed, was the easy part. Getting them to court to face trial was far harder. Having to jump through hoops, making sure the evil scum in front of them had their human rights looked after. That was what stuck in his throat. The scum that passed through every police station in the land did not give their victims' rights a second thought.

Roger Young had sat there in front of them with his solicitor, holding court, knowing that he was not going anywhere but to prison, making them sweat for every ounce of information he could be bothered to impart. That was until Sandall dropped the bombshell they had up their sleeve. The CPS had given the them the go-ahead to charge Young for the murders of Samantha Field and Alison Grant, while they continued their investigation.

-X-

Monteith stuck his head around the door leading into Jimmy Russell's office. The coast was clear.

Where would the files be kept?

Jimmy's computer?

He slipped past the large sofa and chairs to open the door in the far corner of the office. It was locked of course.

Monteith removed a small pouch from his pocket, containing his Jack Knife multi-tool lock pick set. In no time at all he'd opened the door and, switching on the light, stood before him were ten filing cabinets leaning against the three walls that were shaped like a horseshoe.

-X-

Ray steered the Range Rover Evoke around the roundabout that led off the parkway and onto the road towards the casino. He could hear the Russells in animated discussion over Lex. They did on occasion ask what Ray's thoughts were, but the final decision was theirs and God help anyone who stood in their way.

-X-

Monteith knew he had to move quickly to find the files he needed. The employees' ones were kept at the back of the room and he had them in his hands faster than a rabbit could drop down a hole. They were in alphabetical order, making his seize easier. He found Ray's in the bottom drawer of the cabinet marked A-L. Taking it out, Monteith snapped pictures of each relevant page using the camera on his phone, before placing the file back where he'd found it. Lex's was in the next cabinet. He did the same with his. And soon, he had everything he needed.

-X-

Ray pulled the Range Rover Evoke into the reserved parking space behind the casino. Jimmy vacated the car, spotting Monteith's BMW 1 series.

'You would have thought with what we paid him, he would have changed his car by now,' Jimmy said, laughing jokingly to the other two.

-X-

Monteith shut the cabinet one final time, and made for the door. But something caused him to turn back and re-open it. Inside, he found his own file and what he saw within it chilled him to the core. His knees turned to jelly and his head span. Pulling himself together he took a photograph of the piece of A4 paper, replaced the file, locked both cabinets and ensured the cupboard door was shut. As he closed the door to Jimmy's office, he heard the Russells' voices close by, and nipped into the toilet as they rounded the corner.

Ray was leaving the CCTV operations room as he exited.

'Wondered where you had gone,' Ray said, looking at Monteith a little longer than necessary. 'You don't look well.'

'Bad gut from a takeaway I bought on the way home last night,' Monteith lied.

'Boss wants to see you to discuss last night. Wants your input over what to do with Lex.'

'Me?'

'Yeah. You'd better shift it, he's waiting.'

CHAPTER FORTY-EIGHT

Watson sat in the passenger seat alongside DCI Wright, staring out of the window. Following the hectic couple of days they'd had, this home visit was the worst part.

'We need to make sure that what we were told is correct before we talk to Monteith,' Wright said, while trying to negotiate the city centre rush-hour traffic which was becoming a nightmare.

'Joseph Clayton is part of the old brigade. One of a kind. If he doesn't know about it, it's not worth knowing. Call this visit a history lesson. Joseph has lung cancer. Looks like he wants to set records straight.'

They entered the Thelwell estate, passing the sign that read: Welcome to Hell, the hostel where Ronald Freeman had stayed before his murder by his previous DCI. Watson noticed the manager, Sheila Evans, talking to the lookout kids outside in the car park. Both waved at each other as they drove past.

'Friend of yours?' Wright asked.

'Everybody wants to be your friend until they get caught for something they should not be doing.'

Wright pulled up outside Joseph Clayton's house.

Davy's battered Vauxhall Vectra was parked on the drive. As they trod towards the door it opened to reveal Davy. He stood there, blocking the entrance with his bulk.

'Hello Davy, is your father in?' Watson asked.

'What the fuck do you want?' Davy spat, folding his arms across his chest.

'Got a nice way with words this one,' Wright added.

'Don't worry. His bark is worse than his bite.'

'Who's the skirt?' Davy asked, with disgust in his voice.

'My boss, and her bite is worse than her bark.' Watson drew closer to Davy. 'Let us in.'

Davy reluctantly turned back into the house, leaving the door open for them to follow.

Joseph Clayton appeared from the kitchen as both Wright and Watson came into the front room. He walked slowly with the aid of his cane.

'Mr Watson, how nice it is to see you,' Joseph said.

'Evening Joseph, sorry to come round unannounced. This is my boss DCI Tanya Wright. Boss this is Joseph Clayton.'

'Enchante,' Joseph said, as he took Wright's hand and kissed it.

'Cut the flannel, Joseph,' Watson joked, as he sat on the sofa next to DCI Wright.

'Manners cost nothing, Mr Watson,' Joseph said, before easing himself into his chair near the fire, placing the cane within easy reach. 'Davy, tea for everyone please.'

Davy mumbled something under his breath and made his way into the kitchen.

'I take it this is not a social call?'

'No. We'd like to know how you learned about Monteith's heritage, providing it's true of course.'

Joseph stared out of the window. 'Neither of you are from here are you?'

Both Watson and Wright shook their heads.

'I am local born and bred, so was my father, and his father. The expansion in the 1970s brought people from far and wide, mostly from the south, wanting to escape the cities for a quieter way of life. But with the moneyed infrastructure and factory work came the crime. I'm not saying it didn't already exist, it's just that with he influx of outsiders the not so savoury sort arrived. The Russells were one of those families.'

Joseph stopped talking as Davy brought in the drinks and set them down on the coffee table. He handed Joseph his cup, which he put on a side table. Davy then sat himself down on the chair under the window as his old man continued.

'Everybody knew everybody's business before the expansion, you'd even be on first name terms with your local bobbies, not that there were a lot of them. They knew your business and, providing you kept your nose clean, they would leave you alone. They got involved if there were any turf wars or pub punch-ups, but they were few and far between. If something did happen it was usually due to outsiders. The locals wouldn't shit on their own doorsteps.' Joseph stopped and took a swig of his drink.

Wright went to say something but Watson put his hand on her arm and shook his head. 'Just let him talk. Think of this as a history lesson,' he whispered.

She rolled her eyes but let him continue.

'The Russells arrived with the first wave of new arrivals. Malcolm and Betty, with their two sons Jimmy and Allan. They set up home on this estate a couple of streets away. The Monteiths arrived about a month later, Bill and Susan. Susan was pregnant with their firstborn, David.'

Watson looked puzzled. 'I did not know Keith had a brother? He's not mentioned him.'

'You wouldn't,' Joseph said. 'He died age two, before Keith was born. Fell over while he was playing in the garden and cracked his head on the concrete step. Knocked Bill and Susan for six and nearly finished their marriage. Bill wanted to try again for another but Susan didn't. She withdrew into herself. He started working nights with Preston Trucks just to get out of the house while Susan suffered. About a year later she was pregnant again, but word got around the baby wasn't Bill's.' He stopped and looked at them both.

'Malcolm Russell,' Watson sighed.

Joseph smiled back.

'Does Keith know?' Wright asked.

'I don't know. Bill and Susan were ecstatic with the pregnancy. Smothered Keith when he was born and covered him in the preverbal cotton wool. He wanted for nothing. You were in the same school year Mr Watson?'

'Yes,' he confirmed.

'That's right. There were you two, Jimmy and Allan in the two years above you, and my two below.'

'Did Bill ever learn that Keith was not his?' Wright pressed.

'I believe so. He went to have it out with Malcolm Russell and got knocked out for his trouble after threatening the man. Like I said, the Russells are not to be messed with. Davy found that out at school when he told a teacher about Jimmy's playground sweet scam. Ended up with a broken nose and a cut eye, didn't you?'

Davy just laughed. 'It was worth it, as Russell got the cane and he was forced to shut up shop.'

Watson pondered Joseph's motivation.

'Why wait till now to share with us what you knew?'

'Lung cancer,' Joseph replied. Docs have given me three months at most.'

'Dad's not been well for a while. He refused treatment, what with his age,' Davy added.

Wright and Watson took their leave soon after Joseph's bombshell. They had no confirmation that Monteith was the Russell brother's half-brother, but it did not matter whether Monteith knew about his family connection and had chosen not to inform the police when he'd joined the force, or he had no idea they were related, the fact was Monteith could no longer work the case. It jeopardised it. They had to, somehow, bring down the Russell Empire without the CPS finding out.

CHAPTER FORTY-NINE

Katie Monteith settled down in front of the television with her mother, after Rebecca and Pixie had been tucked up in bed for the night. Her mind still whirred following her husband's visit on Wednesday, when he'd told her that his arsehole of a boss had made him choose between going undercover or being booted out of the force, and having to work for the Russells.

Her mother brought two cups of tea in from the kitchen, handing one to her before sitting down in her chair. 'Have you made up your mind yet on what you're going to do?' Katie's mother asked, after taking a sip of her tea.

'I don't know. Stop asking me, Mum. I can't make any long-term decisions, especially with a headache.' She climbed out of the chair and went into the kitchen to the medicine cabinet. Taking two paracetamol she swallowed them down with some water before re-entering the interview room to continue her mother's interrogation.

'You were all set to divorce that thing you call a husband until he came round with that sob story and you have fallen for it, hook, line and sinker.'

'His name is Keith. He is the father of your two

grandchildren, who are upstairs right now, so will you keep your voice down.'

'The only thing he has done right is produce two lovely children. The rest of your marriage has been a shambles from the start.' Her barbed comment wounded Katie. 'How many more times are you going to believe what he says about giving up gambling. He's an addict. He's gambled your money away so you could not go on that holiday to Spain. He's had his car attacked. He's got so much in debt that he owed money to the biggest crooks in the city.'

Katie gave her mother a look of surprise.

'Hey, I'm not just a doddery old widow living on her own, I know what goes on. Word gets about. We don't talk about knitting patterns and baking cakes at the community centre you know. So what cock and bull story has he come up with this time?'

Katie gave her mum the unfiltered version of what Monteith had told her.

'Addicts are liars, love.'

As she climbed the stairs to bed an hour later, she found Rebecca sitting at the top of them.

'Have you been arguing over Dad again?' she asked.

Katie could see that Rebecca had been crying, which meant she must have overheard everything.

She coaxed her back to her bedroom and lay beside her, where she drifted off to sleep.

-X-

Monteith sat staring at the CCTV monitors in front of him, his mind elsewhere. Friday night's and the weekends were their busiest. Tonight was no exception. The casino floor was rammed full of punters handing over their hard-earned cash to the

Russell brothers. But the more customers they had meant he had more trouble to look out for. The security guards downstairs had already thrown out five drunks who didn't know when to quit when it came to trying to chat up the female bar staff or try to kick and punch the fruit machines after having lost all their money. To top it off, one player had been caught counting the cards during a game of blackjack.

Monteith's phone beeped with a text message from Watson.

BBQ at my place tomorrow at 12 p.m. Everyone will be there. Bring Katie and the girls.

Monteith dropped his phone back into his pocket and looked down on the Russell brothers shaking hands with the rich, infamous and corrupt by the restaurant and felt sick. Ray had told him the reason they had visited Don Spedding. At least the council had the balls to stand up against them for once, even though Spedding had ended up in hospital. The thought of the Russells' Gentleman's Club, where they could fleece their clients and use the video recordings as evidence of their presence for leverage was downright abhorrent. But what turned Monteith's stomach was the knowledge that he might be related to them, according to what he'd read in his file. Why had no-one told him? And how could he broach the subject with the Russells? He couldn't exactly ask them outright could he? Not without divulging how he'd discovered the information.

CHAPTER FIFTY

SATURDAY 12 p.m.

The heat was building as Monteith walked up the drive to Watson's front door. He recognised both his and Sally's cars, but the other two parked on the road outside were new to him. As he knocked, Sally opened the door wide.

'Hello, stranger,' she said.

Monteith kissed her on the cheek and gave her a hug. 'No Katie and the girls?'

'No. I asked Katie if she wanted to come, but no deal. Things are still very fragile between us two. She did ask if you could meet her next week though.'

'I will give her a ring tomorrow,' Sally promised, as she closed the door. 'Go through to the kitchen. Everyone's in there.'

Monteith entered the kitchen and stopped dead in the doorway. Watson was standing there wearing his Meatloaf T-shirt but it was the other two guests which took him by surprise. DCI Wright in a floral dress and Superintendent Matthews in a crisp shirt, tie, and blazer.

'Hi, feller, What do you want to drink?' Watson asked, wearing a big grin.

'A beer please,' Monteith replied cautiously, while

nodding to both Wright and Matthews.

'Good to see you,' Matthews said, as he put his hand out. Monteith shook it, still wondering what was happening. He noticed Monteith's hesitation. 'Don't worry Keith. We wanted to see how you were coping.' Turning to Watson he nodded. 'Your office?'

Watson handed Monteith a bottle of San Miguel and winked before opening the door. They all traipsed in, with Watson sitting down at his computer. Matthews shut the door and stood guard. Wright and Monteith sat on two wooden chairs next to each other.

'Keith, something has come to light that we thought you should know about. Which is why we are meeting here and not at work because we don't want this to go around the station.'

Monteith looked confused and concerned. 'I wanted to speak to you as well. Things have gone on this week, which has risked my being discovered. I know they are testing my allegiance to them but I am starting to get worried about my safety.'

'Thanks to your information-gathering, up till now we were building an excellent evidence file to bring the Russell empire to an end. We have also received other information from a source which will help us, but there is something that could jeopardise what we've garnered.'

'Okay . . . ?'

Watson opened a drawer in his desk, pulled out an envelope and handed it to Wright. She opened it and took out the paperwork.

'This information has stayed just between us three and Joseph Clayton who gave it to us, and that's where we want it to stay.'

Wright handed the envelope to Monteith who read it aloud. 'Keith Monteith is half brother to Jimmy and

Allan Russell.' He glanced at her. 'Where did you say you got this from?' he asked.

'Joseph Clayton gave it to me,' Watson said. 'That piece of paper is photocopied from a book he has listing things that the Russells have been involved in since their dad was around.'

'Is there any truth in it?' Wright asked.

There was a knock on the door.'

'Yes?'

'Just to let you know that your other guests are arriving, and are wondering where you are,' Sally said.

'Thanks, love, we won't be much longer,' Watson called out.

'Yesterday, while the Russells and their goons were out, I took the chance to do some "research" in the employees' files. On my phone are some pictures I snapped from Lex and Ray's files.' Monteith had a swig of his beer. 'Also on there are photos of what the Russells had on my file. One of them is of what looks like a copy of my birth certificate, according to which, Malcolm Russell is my dad. I have never seen this before so I don't know if it's genuine. The one I have has both my parents on it, God rest their souls.'

What reason would either of them have for lying about his genetics? And how would they have been able to get hold of a fake birth certificate? Wouldn't having created one caused problems in the background checks the police made prior to Monteith joining the force?

Matthews was looking through Monteith's phone. 'Keith, what you have here is gold dust. Send these over to me, Wright and Watson then delete them from your phone. We can retrieve the deleted files later, but we don't want one of the brothers getting hold of your phone and finding those photos.'

CHAPTER FIFTY-ONE

The Saturday afternoon sun glinted off the surface of the river, with the branches from the overhanging bushes dipping into the water, looking like they were drinking directly from it.

Up on the patio, Jimmy Russell sat looking through his binoculars at the birds floating by. Occasionally using them to check out the house across the river from where he stood. Concentrating on the wife of the family who sunbathed topless on days like this. She knew he was watching her and gave Jimmy a good view of her tanned body. A body which Jimmy knew every inch of, as they had been seeing each other on the side for six months now. Her husband worked abroad in banking for two weeks each month. Jimmy had got to know them after they had dined at his restaurant when the directors were entertaining foreign guests.

'Admiring the view again?' Allan stood by his brother shielding his eyes from the sun's glare.

'I never thought birdwatching was such a great hobby,' Jimmy replied, gazing longingly at the woman's full frontal plumage.

'Bollocks. You used to stare at Diane Butcher across the road when you were fifteen with a small set of binoculars,' Allan reminded Jimmy as he poured himself a coffee.

'I didn't hear you telling me off at the time. You got an eyeful as well, if I remember rightly.'

'Well, watching her get changed with the bedroom curtains open was better than watching television.'

Jimmy could not remember how many women he had been to bed with over the years. Diane Butcher being the first as a seventeenth birthday present. Their late father, Malcolm, had also enjoyed the female form from time to time. Their mother, Betty, didn't do anything to stop him, and even if she had tried, he would get violent. Jimmy had followed in his footsteps.

It was the offshoot of one of their father's liaisons thirty-odd years ago, that they were discussing.

'We need to restructure and be more forceful with those who are against us. We are getting slack in our way and becoming soft with people,' Jimmy commented looking down at the iPad in his hand.

'Well, Don Spedding certainly got the message,' Allan reminded him.

'I'm not talking about business interests. They look after themselves once we put our people in. Don was a pain in the arse who could not do his job properly. We need to see if those around us are really on our side. Tommy Burke wasn't, so we had to get rid of him. There are a number of others who also need to be relieved of their duty.'

'Got anybody in mind?'

'The bar takings have been down over the last two weeks so I put a camera out the back.' Jimmy handed the iPad to Allan, so that he could see the footage on the screen.

'When are they working next?'

'There last shift will be tonight.'

'Who else have you got your eye on?'

'I have a few others. Lex, Monteith, and Ray being three of them. We need to redistribute their roles. Monteith is wasted sat in that office every night. Bruce can do his job, free Monteith up to do other, more worthwhile things.'

Before Allan could press his brother on what he had planned, Ray declared his presence.

Jimmy left his chair, said, 'We'll discuss it later, at the casino,' then patted Allan on the shoulder.

CHAPTER FIFTY-TWO

SUNDAY MORNING

Watson's alcohol-induced headache had not subsided by the time Simon's first game had kicked off.

The manager, Nick Thomas, out of earshot of Simon told Watson that the manager of West Ravenswood's under fourteens was watching from a distance so not to put pressure on Simon and teammate Lance Brewster. Nick nodded towards a smartly dressed man standing on the grass behind one of the goalposts.

Sally, Jason, and Rachael had come along to cheer Simon on. Sally took Rachael to the play area before the match started, leaving Watson and Jason on the touchline talking to the other parents. As they talked Watson noticed a group of teenage boys and girls dressed in tracksuits gathering across the park. They started to do stretches. There trainer called them over as they were running on the spot.

Sally and Rachael joined them back on the touchline, as both teams took up their positions for the start of the match. Watson looked towards the man, who was making notes on an iPad.

The first fifteen minutes were littered with mistakes by both teams as the magnitude of the match got to them. Watson looked at the manager on the grass bank, who had not moved since the start. He glanced at the group of teenage runners. They had finished their first sprint and were stopping for a break to swig on bottles of water. The trainer was going around speaking to them, but something set Watson's police antenna on alert. It was the trainer's demeanour around the girls, getting close to them as he talked and occasionally touching them. A hand on the shoulder here, a light stroke of the arm there.

Sally nudged Watson in time for him to see Normanton take the lead, the ball crossing the line towards the goal. The Ryland players started arguing between themselves while the Normanton players ran off celebrating. Simon began encouraging his teammates to get their minds back on the game, which they did and didn't concede again before half-time.

The difference in the two sides at half-time was poles apart. Normanton's players were hyped up and buzzing. Their manager was as excited as if they had won the match. Their parents too, seemed pleased with their game. On the other side of the pitch, Nick stood in front of the Ryland players, who sat on the ground listening to him. He appeared to be coaching them into a more positive mindset.

The manager of West Ravenswood under fourteens had left his viewpoint and had joined the crowd on the sidelines.

Coming back from the tea bar, Watson spotted a man in a car he recognized. Excusing himself from Sally he wandered over to the man.

'Morning Jeff,' Watson said to DI Jeff Johnson, the detective from the county police force. 'What brings you onto our patch?'

After shaking hands, Jeff nodded his head in the

direction of the athletics trainer. 'You know we have been following Ian Fellows for some time. We have corroborative evidence of his behaviour towards the female runners at the club.'

'We were going to have a word with him regarding a case we have just closed, but after speaking to you the other day we have put it on hold.'

'The Alison Grant and Samantha Field one. Yes, that was good work getting Roger Young. Where did Fellows fit in?'

'Alison was being trained by Fellows and her boyfriend told us about his behaviour. Also, Steph Parkinson said she quit the club because of him.'

'We interviewed Steph Parkinson the other day with her father. Very interesting what she said. So much so, we are picking him up this morning. That's Fellows' car.' Jeff pointed to a Skoda Octavia parked just down the row. 'We have been videoing his training this morning for more evidence. We should be done before your football match is finished.'

'I will watch the fireworks then.' Watson shook hands with Jeff and made his way back to Sally.

The second half began with both teams vying for the upper hand. The Ryland team did just that seven minutes in. Simon caught the ball and their striker ran it through the Normanton defence, taking his time to draw the keeper out. Who slipped the ball under him and into the net, despite the goal keepers efforts.

The Ryland team and their parents went crazy with elation. The team jumped on the striker and soon they were all in a heap. Cheers and glee-filled shouts of encouragement filled the field.

'Good through-pass from your lad.' Watson turned to find the West Ravenswood manager standing beside him.

'Thank you.' Waston introduced himself to the manager, who said his name was Thomas Park. He kept his eye on Fellows as they spoke. The training session ended halfway through the second half of the match. Fellows packed up his stuff and made his way back to his car, continuing his over-friendliness towards a few of his young female coachees as he crossed the field.

Watson stood back from the crowd, holding the man in his sight from the car park. As Fellows started to drop his equipment into the boot of his car, Jeff and his partner walked over to him as a squad car turned the corner, blocking his car in. Fellows tried to make a run for it but was caught, handcuffed and put in the back of the squad car. A crowd had gathered as Fellows was driven away. Jeff looked up as he opened his car door, spotting Watson, he waved and got in.

The match became a battle of attrition. Both teams refusing to give an inch in their determination to avoid relegation. Ryland had the upper hand by drawing, Normanton had to score but were coming up against a Lance Brewster-led defence.

With three minutes to go, Ryland's winger was given a free kick near the right-hand side of the Normanton penalty area. The ball landed in the penalty area, a Normanton defender head-butted the ball, sending it towards Simon. Everything seemed to go into slow motion as Simon took aim. He kicked the ball with his right foot, watching it arrow through the players in front of him. It glanced off the inside of the post and nestled in the top corner of the net.

It took a couple of seconds for it to register what had just happened before euphoria exploded. The Ryland players shot off after Simon, who was wheeling away after the goal towards the parents, his arm outstretched in a hero's celebration.

He was at the halfway line before they caught and jumped on him. Some of the Normanton players collapsed in tears, while others pleaded with the referee to disallow the goal for having gone offside to no avail.

Sally jumped into Watson's arms in delight. Jason and Rachael were running around screaming in delight. Thomas Park wore a huge smile on his face.

Watson's headache had dulled to a bearable thud.

CHAPTER FIFTY-THREE

MONDAY, 6 a.m.

Early morning raids were part and parcel of the job.

Sandall and Lorimer were sitting in Watson's car, who was ready to issue the order to 'go'. The ARU were positioned ready as the three of them alighted from the car. Superintendent Matthews had signed off on the raid while at the BBQ after the pow-wow in Watson's office.

Lorimer signalled to the lead officer, and the impolite sound of the door caving in under the impact of the enforcer could be heard from where they stood.

'Police!' echoed down the hallway of the terraced house, as armed officers entered the property, splitting in groups of two to cover both floors. The downstairs rooms were given the all-clear as Watson and Lorimer headed upstairs – where they found who they were after. He was lying on the floor by the bed, beneath two burly officers who were cuffing him.

His female companion was trying to cover up her naked body on the bed. The young woman looked no older than seventeen.

The officers managed to pull him upright just as

Watson entered the bedroom. 'Get the young lady some clothes. She can come with us as well,' Watson ordered a uniformed officer. He didn't know where to look never mind how to get the woman off the bed. The young woman gathered her skimpy-looking clothes and bolted out of the door into the waiting arms of another officer.

Watson stood in front of the man they had come for. 'Alex John Sullivan you are under arrest for the murder of Wayne Marsh . . .' He continued to read Lex his rights under a torrent of abuse. 'Get him dressed.' Watson finished, before turning and going back downstairs to find Sandall. He was in the front room.

'If you find anything related to the Russells, bag it. We cannot leave a single stone unturned.'

Sandall nodded and continued to search the property.

Watson came back out into the hall as Lex was brought downstairs, dressed in a tracksuit. Lex looked over the banister, 'When I get released I know where you live and I'm coming after your family.'

'I've heard it all before Lex. It'll be a long time before you see the outside again, get him out of here,' Watson said, dismissively.

-X-

MONDAY, 10 a.m.

Monteith sat down on the green leather sofa in Jimmy Russell's office, wondering why he had been called in so early. Jimmy and Allan were in the two leather chairs across from him on the other side of the large glass coffee table. He knew the first part of the takedown had happened, with Lex's arrest. Now he was putting part two into action.

'Keith,' Jimmy started, 'you have been with us for almost two months. We just wanted a chat to see how you are doing.'

'Erm, it's going okay apart from having been abducted, being forced to give up my career in the force–'

'We went through all that with you when you came to work for us.'

'Made to work for you!' Monteith snapped.

'Nobody made you come here; we just pointed out the ramifications if you didn't.'

Monteith shot up off the sofa.

'I've not finished!' Jimmy's voice was as hard as his stare.

Monteith shot glances at both the brothers before slowly sitting back down.

Jimmy continued, 'The reason we have asked you to come in is that we are planning to expand the business and we'd like you to help us to do it.' Jimmy looked at Allan, who removed a wad of paper from inside his jacket pocket.

Monteith picked up the contract and studied it.

'Why me?'

'You're family.'

'No, I'm not.'

'You are our half-brother whether you like it or not. The birth certificate in your possession might say something different but the real one, we have in ours, says otherwise. We share the same biological father.'

He hoped they believed the expression of surprise he wore.

'Why do you think we tried to help you when your gambling got out of hand?' Jimmy asked. 'We saw how out of hand it was getting and had to do something about it. Banning you from the tables and getting you to repay your debts was the only course of action, brother.'

'Why was I not told?'

'I don't know.' Jimmy shrugged. 'I do remember when I was about six your father having a big row with our dad.'

An out of breath Ray came through the door. 'Boss.'

'Can't you see we are in a meeting?'

'Lex has been arrested. I went to pick him up and the road was sealed off with police. Spoke to someone who said there was an early morning raid and a man fitting Lex's description had been carted off, along with a young woman.'

'Can't he keep it in his pants?' Jimmy jumped up from his chair.

He turned to Monteith. 'You have any contacts in the force you can trust?'

'I burned a lot of bridges by coming to work for you. Most of them still want my guts for garters, they certainly are no longer talking to me. Why?' Monteith asked, already having guessed.

'Find out why Lex has been arrested, and what's he has been saying. We need to cover our arses in case he turns snitch. Ray, you go with him.'

CHAPTER FIFTY-FOUR

The alarm sounded from the interview room, bringing every officer available to the assistance of Watson and Lorimer. Four officers came flying through the door where Lex could be seen, holding his solicitor by the collar up against the wall. It took all of them to grapple him off the man and re-cuff him.

'Are you alright?' Watson asked, the solicitor, Colin Roberts, as he sat back down to watch the officers escort Lex from the room and march him back to his cell.

'Yes. Don't think he wants to co-operate,' Roberts replied, stuffing his paperwork back in his bag. 'I will speak to him later, when he has calmed down.'

'Good luck with that,' Lorimer said.

Lorimer directed Roberts to the canteen, as he and Watson made their way towards the incident room.

'That was quick?' Wright said, looking at her watch.

'Lex attacked his solicitor before his interview could begin.'

'It's his time he is wasting, not ours. With the footage we have of Lex forcing the tablets down

Wayne Marsh's throat and the CCTV footage of him dumping Wayne's body in the park, the CPS have already given us the go-ahead to charge him.'

Watson's mobile phone rang as Wright reached her desk.

'Meet you at the place,' Monteith said.

'See you there,' Watson replied.

-X-

The drive to the rendezvous point gave Monteith a chance to glean more information from Ray, while he drove the log way.

'How long have you worked for Jimmy and Allan then?' Monteith asked, as he pulled into traffic, heading for the city centre.

'About five or six years, I think. Started in security, like you.'

'It that your forte? What you did before?'

'Yes, had my own company after coming out of the army. Sold it when the regulations got too tight, cost too much to keep it viable with all the red tape the government wanted it wrapped up in.'

Monteith eased out of the traffic and took the turning towards Copeland.

'So what has Jimmy Russell got on you?' Monteith glanced at Ray. 'You know mine is my gambling, and Lex's is probably something from his time in London. What's yours?'

Ray looked at Monteith then back out of the windscreen. 'There was a fight at a local nightclub where I was working on security. A drug dealer died. Jimmy killed him. I saw him do it. He said I would end up the same way if I told the old bill. When the police arrived I gave them a false description of the culprit. Then when I sold the company Jimmy gave me a job.'

'So he bought your silence.'

Ray didn't reply.

Monteith swung the car into an industrial estate, and parked behind Watson's Ford Focus.

'We're here,' Monteith said, as Watson got out of his car and into the back of Monteith's BMW.

'You know if I'm seen speaking to you, I'm done for. Your name is mud back at the station,' Watson said angrily. He pointed to Ray. 'Who the fuck is this?' he asked for good measure.

'Don't get on your high horse. You didn't have to see me, you could have told me to fuck off like the rest of them. This is Ray, works for the Russells.'

'Hello Ray, you're under arrest,' Watson started, flashing the man his ID card.

'Fuck off.' Ray opened the door and got halfway out, walking straight into Lorimer, who spun him round and pushed him against the side of the car, grabbing his wrists in the process to apply a set of handcuffs as he cautioned him, before handing him to a uniformed constable who would drive him to the custody suite.

CHAPTER FIFTY-FIVE

Wright stood watching the happenings on the monitors inside the CCTV operations room with a view to both Ray and Lex's interviews, which were miraculously occurring simultaneously.

Watson and Sandall were with Lex, Lorimer and French sat opposite Ray.

'Lex,' Watson asked, 'do you know of a man named Wayne Marsh?'

'You know I do,' Lex replied, relaxing in his chair, arms folded. His solicitor had informed him prior to the preliminary introductions following his caution that if he pulled any more crap he'd be on his own. He was behaving himself so far.

'How do you know Wayne Marsh?'

'He was hanging around the casino selling drugs,' Lex said, impassively.

Watson opened the file on the table in front of him and brought out a photo. 'I am showing Lex Sullivan evidence number AS1. 'Who is this a photograph of?'

'Wayne Marsh.'

'Mr Marsh died shortly after this image was captured on one of the cameras inside the casino. Do you know anything about his death?'

Lex looked at his solicitor, straightened his spine and said, 'Yes, I killed Wayne Marsh – but it was on the order of another person.'

Watson looked at Sandall. This corroborated what Monteith had told them. 'Who instructed you to murder Wayne?'

Lex looked again at his solicitor, who nodded he assent to answer. 'Allan Russell.'

'How, exactly?'

'He said: "you know what to do" and handed me the bags of ecstasy we had taken from Wayne.'

'What did you take that to mean?'

'That he wanted me to get rid of Wayne by giving him the ecstasy.'

'Feeding him the pills?'

'Yes.'

-X-

Monteith's phone rang as he came to stand beside Wright. He removed it from his pocket and scanned the number on the screen.

'Jimmy Russell, wondering what is happening I expect.'

Wright grinned. 'Let him sweat. We have eyes on him. He's not going anywhere.'

-X-

'Answer the fucking phone,' Jimmy shouted at his mobile, as if Monteith could hear him, before slamming it down on his desk. 'Where the hell are they?' He shot a look at Allan. 'I don't like this. Lex gets arrested and now we cannot get hold of Keith or Ray.'

Their father, Malcolm, had instilled in them the

need to have complete control over everything they did, that way they'd know what was going on at all times. Right now, Jimmy felt powerless. He stood to pour himself a drink, spinning a decanter in front of Allan's face, he asked if he wanted one.

Allan shook his head.

'His phone might just be out of range,' Allan said in a placating tone.

'What, Ray's too?' Jimmy mocked.

'No, you're right. It's iffy.'

'Iffy?' Jimmy asked, incredulously. 'It fucking stinks.'

CHAPTER FIFTY-SIX

During recess, the team gathered in the conference room for a brief on the imminent arrest of the Russell brothers.

Kendall spoke first. 'We've got Allen for ordering Wayne Marsh's murder, and he and Jimmy for Monteith's abduction, the council worker Don Spedding's attack and their previous security chief, Tommy Burke's assault. And with Lex and Ray tweeting, he's going to be doing bird for a long while.'

'What about the things Joseph Clayton wrote down?' Wright asked.

'I've confirmed a drug dealer by the name of Jason King, aka Big K, was murdered at a nightclub where Ray worked as a security guard,' Kendall said. 'I've also managed to find a witness willing to testify against Allan, who reckons he was present when a derelict building went up in flames. Says Allan had threatened to torch it when squatters moved in. Two of them died.'

'Right,' Matthews said, 'let's move.'

The convoy made its way out of the city centre towards the Russells' casino. Watson and Monteith in the lead, with Lorimer, Sandall and French following behind. Kendall and the arrest team were in a marked Ford Transit a few vehicles back so as not to arouse suspicion.

'Good to have you back with us,' Watson said, glancing at Monteith.

Monteith was just thinking of a witty remark when his phone rang.

'It's Jimmy – again.'

'Tell him you are on your way back.'

-X-

'Finally,' Jimmy said, sliding his phone into his pocket. The brothers had made their way down to the casino floor to welcome their visitor.

'Mr Grant, thank you for coming at short notice.' Jimmy held out his hand for David Grant to shake.

'Mr Russell, *I* should be thanking *you*, *and* your brother of course,' Grant replied, shaking Allan's hand. 'Your interest in financing my company is overwhelming.'

'Please take a seat.' Jimmy directed their visitor to the lounge inside the bar.

Once they were settled and both had drinks in front of them, Jimmy continued. 'First, my condolences on the loss of your daughter, I read about it in the paper. When is the funeral?'

Grant swallowed hard, 'Thank you,' he said. 'It's next week.'

'Well, please send us the bill. We'd be only too glad to cover the cost,' Jimmy said.

David Grant choked back his tears, 'I couldn't let you do that.'

'It's the least we can do, partner.'

'Thank you, sir,' Grant said.

'Mr Grant, we've given it a lot of thought, and we

feel that Argent Logistics could do with our help. We have been looking to expand into distribution for some time and your company would be the perfect way to start. Using your experience in the field and our money and contacts to back it, we can expand your enterprise.'

Allan smiled inwardly, watching his brother in action. Negotiating was his forte. He reached into a file and brought out a raft of paperwork, which he placed on the table in front of Mr Grant. 'Please survey the contract we have had written up and, if you are happy, sign here, here and here,' Allan emphasised his words with the end of the ballpoint pen as he nodded to Jimmy.

'I wouldn't sign anything if I were you, Mr Grant,' Watson bellowed from the end of the room.

Monteith walked across the floor towards the table, closely followed by Lorimer, Sandall, and French. They had come in through the staff entrance that had been mapped out by Monteith for their perusal as they'd assembled the team during their briefing fifteen minutes before. Kendall and the other uniforms were guarding all the exits.

'What the fuck has it got to do with you?' Grant's anger went from zero to a hundred in less than a second.

Jimmy and Allan stood in front of the two plain-clothed detectives, the rage visibly building on their faces. 'Keith, what the hell is going on? Where is Ray?'

Monteith and Watson produced their ID cards, Monteith indicating to Watson with a tilt of his head that he was going to do the honours. 'Ray and Lex are back at the station helping us with our inquiries. Jimmy and Allan Russell, you are both under arrest.'

Grant shot up out of his seat and launched himself at Watson. 'You couldn't stop my daughter from being killed, now you want to ruin my business!' He managed to punch him on the arm before Lorimer and Sandall both grabbed Grant and dragged him to the floor, cuffing him. 'I am arresting you for assaulting a police officer...'

Jimmy and Allan took advantage of the distraction and made a run for it, but were caught in the doorway by PC Kendall. They doubled back and headed into the restaurant, dodging cleaners and other personnel.

Monteith ran after them.

The men threw chairs to block their pursuit and detoured into the kitchen, only to come face to face with two police officers. Picking up a carving knife and a boning knife the two turned back into the restaurant, finding themselves cornered by Watson and Monteith.

'Why are you running? We only want to ask you a few questions back at the station?' Monteith tried to calm down the situation before escalation.

'You lied to us, Keith,' Jimmy said.

'Whatever Lex and Ray have told you it's not true,' Allan added.

'Who said they told us anything? We don't need them to verify that you arranged my abduction; we have them on camera, stuffing me into the van. We've got you, Allan, pulling out of the car park opposite and following the van. We don't need Lex or Ray to help put you away.' He glanced down at the blades they held. 'Do you want to add to your charges?'

EPILOGUE

A WEEK LATER

Watson wandered into the office, his arm still in a sling following the takedown of the Russell brothers. Jimmy had managed to get a swing in with his knife before being tasered, hitting Watson in the upper arm. Allan had been tasered before he'd been able to get a blow in.

He took a seat in Wright's office. He had been called in for a back to work debrief.

'How are you feeling, Terry?' Wright asked, as she put a coffee cup down on the edge of her desk for Watson, before taking a seat opposite him.

'I feel fine, ready to return to work. The arm is still a bit sore and the stitches are due out at the end of the week. Just need your say-so.'

Wright looked at her computer and pressed a few keys. 'Before you can return, you are to see a force approved counsellor and it will be his say on when you will be allowed back. I would love to see you behind your desk tomorrow but I must follow protocol. And with everything you have suffered over the last few months, what with DCI Crompton, your confrontation with the Russells means the powers that be upstairs have decreed you consult a therapist

before starting your official role as DI for the agency.'
Watson nodded, reluctantly.

-X-

The list of charges against the Russell brothers, Lex and Ray were long; as word had spread about their arrest and the inspection of their businesses, chickens had begun coming home to roost. The fraud office had begun sifting through their accounts, and had started interviewing present and former employees of the Russell empire.

Wright, Monteith, and Matthews were in court for Jimmy, Allan and Ray's bail hearings. The smiles were wiped off their faces when they were each told they must remain in prison on remand while awaiting trial.

-X-

Work was underway to find the women that Roger Young had taken and murdered. He was imprisoned, awaiting sentencing for the murders of Alison Grant and Samantha Field. The agency were interviewing him from behind bars about the bodies of Viv Miller and Caroline Dicks who'd been found buried behind Young's farmhouse, in a field he had sold to his neighbour.

During an interview with Monteith and Sandall, with a prison officer guarding the room from the doorway, Young had divulged the whereabouts of two more women he'd murdered.

'I will tell you where Stacey Kitchen and Angela Perry are. I was putting up fences in a village south of here when I came across them. Baxley, I think the place was.' Young leaned back in his chair and took on a relaxed pose. 'There was a new estate being built across from where I was working. They are buried on that estate, but you won't find them without difficulty.'

Monteith and Sandall looked at each other waiting for Young to continue. 'Why?' Sandall asked.

Young leaned forwards, arms on the table. 'Because I buried them beneath two of the houses when the footings had been put in but the concrete had not yet been poured into the foundations to create bases. Now the estate is occupied.'

ACKNOWLEDGEMENTS

I would like to thank Louise, Michael, and everyone else at Dark Edge Press for their hard work in publishing this book. They have made me feel very welcome, and I look forward to continuing to work with them.

I would like to thank Leanne Braithwaite and Caz Bower for editing, proofreading, and bashing the original manuscript into the story you have read.

Jamie Curtis for his great work in designing the covers for my books.

My wife, Ann, Maureen Davis, Beryl Fielder, and Gary Clarke for their help as beta readers.

To Kerrie Watson and Kerry Monteith. The original Watson & Monteith.

Finally, I would like to thank my readers. Thank you for purchasing this book, and I hope you enjoyed It. Please could you leave a review on Amazon, Goodreads, or any other books sites?

Tony has worked as a lifeguard, both here and abroad, a white-van man, a baker, a civil servant for the MOD, and in Children and Adult Social Services for the local council. Ideas for a novel had been floating around in his head for some time before be put pen to paper and began writing his first novel.

Born in Warrington Cheshire in 1967 Tony moved to Rutland in 1981. He now lives in Peterborough with his wife, two nutty cats and a Romanian rescue dog. When not writing he likes to listen to Rock and Heavy Metal. Something he has in common with our Publishing Director.

Love crime fiction as much as we do?

Sign up to our associates program to be first in line to receive Advance Review Copies of our books, and to win stationary and signed, dedicated editions of our titles during our monthly competitions. Further details on our website: www.darkedgepress.co.uk

Follow @darkedgepress on Facebook, Twitter, and Instagram to stay updated on our latest releases.

Printed in Great Britain
by Amazon